That Your Joy May Be Full
A Christopher Book

gift of author

Other Christopher Books

'And You, Who Do You Say I Am?'
Jesus as people experience Him

Enjoy the Lord
A guide to prayer

Young Ideas
Articles written by young people

You Can Still Change the World
How the individual can improve society

What a Day This Can Be!
A "Three Minutes" book

Three Minutes a Day
Volume 20 in the series

Three Minutes a Day
Volume 21 in the series

That Your Joy May Be Full

A Christopher Book

Father John Catoir

Director, The Christophers

THE CHRISTOPHERS, 12 East 48th St., New York, NY 10017

Cover photo by Joseph R. Thomas

Scripture quotations in this publication are from The Words of Jesus, © Jose de Vinck, or the
Revised Standard Version Bible, © National Council of the Churches of Christ in the U.S.A.
and are used with permission.

24061

To Mary the Mother of Jesus—
Cause of our Joy

Acknowledgements

Jesus preached a gospel of love. The purpose of His mission was put very simply: "I have told you all this that your joy may be full."

The gospel of love is an invitation to joyful living. Love in action is service, but service often leads to drudgery. We speak of the cross when the burdens of love become heavy. Tough love is sometimes required of us. At times we are called to involve ourselves in unpleasant confrontations.

Where is the joy in this gospel of love? It certainly takes courage and deep faith to believe that the cross is good, and that joy will prevail over tension and sorrow. It takes a special kind of faith to experience joy in the midst of sorrow.

In my efforts to write a book about joy, to clarify this mysterious word for myself and for you, I have turned to Jesus Christ, trying to understand from His perspective. In the process I've been helped by many friends and associates. I am grateful to them for their encouragement and support.

It is the Christopher tradition to test words and ideas within a committee framework. Portions of this book were written originally in that manner and presented as Christopher News Notes. For that reason I am indebted to current and former members of the Christopher Editorial Committee: Joe Thomas, Dolores Criqui, Jeanne Glynn, Joan Bromfield, Maryanne Sanagorski and Betty Powers Smith. Thanks also to Catherine de Vinck for permission to use her poetry and for her valuable insights in the preparation of this manuscript.

Rev. John Catoir
Easter 1982

Table of Contents

Introduction

Let a person come forward, a living person capable of speaking to the heart; let truth flow from this person's life and let the person's power be matched by an equal gift of love; then people will listen to the Good News, and the dawn of better days will brighten our skies.

Cardinal Duval (pastoral letter)

How I wish I could be such a person for you. Perhaps you'll allow me to try.

It seems to me all of us are seeking the same thing: happiness. We have so much in common. Even though we may have travelled different roads to reach our present state in life, our basic hope is the same: a brighter, happier future. We'd all like to believe the future will be better than anything we've ever known before. The fact is, with the help of God, it will be.

Life on earth is only the beginning of our human existence. We were made for eternal joy. But eternal life doesn't begin after we die, it has already begun. Joy is not only our future destiny it is our Christian vocation.

The word "joy" conjures up images of celebration, full-bodied laughter, or feelings of enchantment. But there is another dimension. Joy is essentially a share in God's inmost Being. God is perfectly whole needing nothing for completion. He possesses in Himself the fullness of Being and Life.

The word "happiness" comes from the Greek and means "without pining"—that is, longing for nothing more. God is completely happy and it is His very nature to share Himself with us. It pleases Him to help us partake of His banquet.

Why, then, is there so much misery in the world? Why can't we learn to live in His joy? Probably because we look for it in the wrong places. When Jesus gave His final discourse at the Last Supper, He said, "It is to the glory of My Father that you should bear much fruit, and then you will be My disciples. As the Father has loved Me, so I have loved you. Remain in My love. If you keep My commandments you will remain in My love, just as I have kept My Father's commandments and remain in His love."

He then put the finishing touch to His public teaching, "I have told you this so that My own joy may be in you and your joy be complete." (Jn. 15:8-12)

It was clearly the intention of Jesus to lead us to joy by revealing a secret hidden from the world. His words have a special power.

When we seek happiness, naturally we are predisposed to follow our own instincts. Often we are misled and deceived in our assessment of how to find true happiness. We are lured by false promises, we take foolish risks.

Let me be specific. Take alcohol as one of the many creature comforts available to us. It seduces the unsuspecting, delivering the very opposite of happiness. The so-called "happy hour" has often led to a bag full of misery. A prose-poem taken from Alcoholics Anonymous makes the point very well.

Positively Negative

We drank for happiness and became unhappy
We drank for joy and became miserable
We drank for sociability and became argumentive
We drank for sophistication and became obnoxious
We drank for friendship and made enemies
We drank for sleep and awakened without rest
We drank for strength and felt weak
We drank medicinally and acquired health problems
We drank for relaxation and got the shakes
We drank for bravery and became afraid
We drank for confidence and became doubtful
We drank to make conversation easier and slurred our
  speech
We drank to feel heavenly and ended up feeling like hell
We drank to forget and were forever haunted
We drank for freedom and became slaves
We drank to erase problems and saw them multiply
We drank to cope with life and invited death.

Anonymous

That's a sad song, isn't it? But the person who wrote it knew what he was talking about.

Drink is only one kind of seduction, there are lots of others. St. Augustine once said, "Sadness always follows worldly joy." I think I understand that. After some selfish indulgence there is momentary joy, a counterfeit joy, but then it evaporates. This experience makes the words of Jesus even more intriguing. If worldly pursuits lead to a state of joylessness, it just might follow that Jesus is right (which of course He is) that spiritual pursuits lead to joy, even when it appears they are the very negation of joy. The words of Jesus are to be trusted.

In the Sermon on the Mount, Jesus said things like, "Happy are they who suffer persecution. . . Happy are they who hunger and thirst for justice. . ." Happiness is not usually associated with suffering and hunger. People tend to withdraw from sacrifice precisely because it appears to narrow their chances for happiness. And in fact it does, temporarily. But the saints have always reflected a radiant joy in spite of the fact that they might be worn out from the strain of self-giving.

We look for joy in the wrong places. Very few of us have the faith to persevere in heroic charity because it costs so much. As a result we miss a great deal of life.

I remember an experience once that filled me with a strange euphoria. I was in Selma, Alabama, with Martin Luther King Jr. during a protest demonstration to secure the voting rights of poor blacks. Our group was surrounded by bands of toughs carrying clubs and yelling profanities. They didn't dare cross the line to strike us because the police were nearby, but tempers were raw. Anything could have happened.

In the midst of that, in the midst of fear and trepidation, I felt an indescribable elation. I've never felt it before or since. But I understood then the mystery of the Beatitudes. A blessed happiness does indeed come to those who take risks for the Lord.

I don't think it's possible to do anything without the deepest possible conviction of God's love. God is never outdone in generosity.

The gospels speak eloquently of His love. In them God reveals Himself. Today there are still some people who communicate with God in a special way. Here are two fairly recent examples from spiritual writers who spoke prophetically to us about God's love. I think you'll see why I chose them. Both are from the journals of contemplative nuns. The first one recorded God's message in these words:

The most important work is not that which you do: it is that which you allow Me to do among you.

Do not worry about the results of your work: it is I who give it growth and fruitfulness in the measure in which it is entrusted to Me.

The more you give Me, the more I will increase your capacity for growing.

Oh how full I am of compassion! And how I desire, I need the generosity of some to make reparation for others.

So many anxieties and shadows in your heart! Think of Me, of Me: perfect Beauty, Splendor, Peace, Life, Truth, Holiness—of Me, your God who loves you.

From *The Spiritual Legacy of Sister Mary of the Holy Trinity* (Louisa Jacques, 1901–1942)

A second religious woman also recorded the words she understood as coming from God:

Always remember that if I love you it is because you are little, not because you are good.

Many souls believe love consists in saying: "My God I love You!" No, love is sweet and acts because it loves; and everything it does is done out of love. I want you to love Me in that way in work, in rest, in prayer and consolation as well as in distress and humiliation, constantly giving

proof of your love by acts. That is true love.
From *The Way of Divine Love*
Sister Josefa Menendez (1890–1923)

Evelyn Underhill, the great authority on mysticism and a spiritual writer, made this interesting comment:

> The spiritual life of the human person does not consist in mere individual betterment or assiduous attention to one's soul, but in a free and unconditional response to the pressure and call of the Holy Spirit, whatever the cost may be. For a spiritual life is simply a life in which all that we do comes from the centre, where we are anchored in God: a life soaked through and through by a sense of His reality and claim, and self-given to the great movement of His will. Christ's whole ministry was an illustration of this mystery.

God is love. My favorite line in Christian literature is this: "The greatest honor you can give to God is to live gladly because of the knowledge of His love." (Juliana of Norwich) Joy is the Christian's natural habitat.

It may not be possible to live gladly all the time. We all have our ups and downs, but thanks to God we have a vision, a faith perception of a loving God which keeps us going. We are a privileged people. Our goal is heaven, and with divine help we can make it; in fact we believe eternal life has already begun here on earth. Let us rejoice in the Risen Lord.

Some people are put off by this emphasis on joy, and I understand that. They know that the real life of the Spirit has little to do with emotional enjoyment sought for its own sake, even if it is enjoyment of the loftiest kind. But that doesn't mean our religion should make us stodgy.

Modern psychology has been promoting an old idea disguised as a new theory, namely that complete self-expression is the condition of a full and happy personal life. When one stops to consider that the spiritual life offers few attractions to the natural pre-dispositions of human nature, then the "complete self-expression theory" is immediately suspect. Self-indulgence does not produce the joy of which I speak.

The will of God invariably leads to a life of discipline and renunciation; a life that seems to cancel all hope for full self-expression. But so what? When you stop to think about it, no one can achieve complete self-expression anyway; not the atheist, not the secular humanist, not the believing Christian, not anyone. Why? Because no one can do or be all the things he or she is capable of doing or being in one lifetime. We have to make choices, and accept our limitations.

To attain any goal we have to develop some faculties or talents at the expense of others. It's impossible to give every one of our talents or interests full expression.

Living gladly because of the knowledge of God's love means that the mind focuses on God, away from the insatiable demands of the tyrannical ego. Focusing on God brings the richest liberation of all. There is a sweetness of spirit that is indescribable in one of God's holy ones. It's really true: the greatest honor you can give to Almighty God is to live gladly because of the knowledge of His love.

The focus is always on God. Otherwise we can very easily become self-centered, driven from within. "I must do this, I must do that."

These are nervous words. No one gets very far in spiritual growth thinking about themselves, and all that they have to do. Joy is not attained through self-indulgence, or a life of religious posturing. It is certainly not found in anxious activity. Joy flows from our relationship with God. Joy comes from the Lord, He communicates it to us. We merely respond to the promptings of His Spirit.

Jesus said, "To see Me is to see the Father." To anchor one's life in God, therefore, is to turn to Jesus. He will unlock the mystery of joy for all of us.

His advice can be stark:

Lay up for yourselves treasures in heaven where neither moth nor rust doth corrupt, and where thieves do not break and enter. . . Seek God first and everything else will be added to you.

(Mt. 6:20, 33)

Jesus taught us to find joy, not by looking for it, but by listening to His words in a spirit of humble surrender.

Enjoyment sought for its own sake is a self-centered pursuit. The Spirit does not teach us to seek joy as an end in itself. Joy is more a by-product of our intimacy with God and this openness to the Lord begins with faith in His love. He loves each of us deeply, passionately, eternally.

This is a book about the gift of joy, but it will not dwell on the word "joy" per se. It will look to Jesus who is the Way, the Truth and the Light. Our joy is intimately connected with Him, and His plans for us.

PART
I

*You have the words
of eternal life*
John 6:68

CHAPTER ONE

A Conversation About Faith

I read your book *Enjoy the Lord* and it gave me a whole new attitude toward the faith. I see better now that Christianity is not an arbitrary code of laws and prohibitions but something more. Can we talk some more about it?

Sure. What's on your mind?

The whole question of faith, I find it very difficult. I mean, I know Christianity is the religion Jesus Christ founded, but there are so many different sects, so much rivalry and contention between them. How do you make sense out of it?

For me, Christianity is an invitation; an invitation to a special kind of happiness and goodness, one that's rooted in the person of Jesus Christ. I don't think about all the division, I try to concentrate on the things that bind us together.

Do you remember His words, "I am the Vine, you are the branches"? (Jn. 15:1) In that image Jesus explains the basic Christian truth that all life and vitality are drawn from God, and that the supreme revelation of God is found in Jesus. Remember, union with God always depends more on His love for us than on our love for Him. That's why God sent Jesus, not for any particular group alone but for the whole human race.

Jesus is not only a spiritual leader, the founder of a religion, He is the Lord of all life. We are called to unite with Him in faith because we are all invited to a banquet of everlasting life. Some may respond, some may not, but God's love is given just the same.

Look, I'm a Christian by birth, a Catholic, but I'm not much of a Catholic and I'm not even sure if I really believe in Jesus Christ, or anything supernatural for that matter. I want to, but I don't understand what faith is.

I think it was Newman who said, "A thousand difficulties do not make one doubt." Faith is a kind of seeing in the dark, so don't be surprised if there's darkness. Faith is basically knowledge. You have the stirrings of faith. You're on the right track. The desire to believe is already a gift. So be patient with yourself.

I think our religion is basically a personal relationship with Jesus; He becomes the central relationship of our lives. As that happens we begin to grow in faith and trust. But be patient. It will come. You're still at the beginning stages.

Why are you a Catholic?

Wow, that's a big question. There are lots of reasons. My family has been Catholic for generations, but that doesn't explain it fully. I almost lost my faith—or thought I did—when I was in college. I had lots of problems with things I saw until I was able to make the distinction between the human and divine elements of the church.

Wherever you have human nature you have sin. So there is sin in the church, lots of it, but I'm a Catholic because of the divine element, because of Jesus Christ, the sacraments, the Eucharist, and much more.

What do you mean?

I see holiness in the Church, holy men and women who have drawn from His life, people who live as Jesus lived.

For instance?

There are millions of them, so many hidden saints; but a few really stand out—Dorothy Day was one I knew and admired.

The last time I spoke to her, she reminded me that I had concelebrated the first Mass offered at the Catholic Worker farm in Tivoli, New York, many years earlier. I mention her because she has been one of the most influential persons in my life.

Sometimes people who criticize the church see only the superficial shell, failing to grasp the greatness within. Extraordinary signs are given in the holiness of people like Dorothy who for more than four decades quietly led a dedicated life in New York's Bowery, where she and her co-workers engaged in feeding the hungry, clothing the naked. She wrote about it regularly in *The Catholic Worker*, her monthly newspaper.

In the June, 1980, issue there was a quote which for me summed up Dorothy's life. "There is no love without the cross, and no cross without a victim. And whether we be on the cross or beneath it weeping, there is Christ, and our sorrow shall be turned to joy."

Over the years *The Catholic Worker* in my judgment has provided some of the best contemporary spiritual reading available in the English language. On the last page of that same issue I found a quote from Archbishop Oscar Romero, who on March 24, 1980, was assassinated in El Salvador for speaking out in behalf of justice. His life had been threatened many times for his defense of the oppressed poor. He wrote the following piece in anticipation of his murder:

> As a Christian I do not believe in death without resurrection. As a pastor I am obliged by Divine mandate to give my life for those I love who are all Salvadorians even those that are going to assassinate me. If they complete their threats, then I offer to God my blood for the redemption and resurrection of El Salvador. Martyrdom is a grace from God that I do not merit. But if God accepts the sacrifice of my life, my blood must be the seed of liberty and a sign of hope that will soon be a reality. . . if they kill me, I forgive and bless those who do it. Yet I hope that they would convince themselves that they are wasting their time; a bishop will die, but the Church of God, that is, the People, will never come to an end.

Now that's a saint!

Dorothy Day and Archbishop Romero are only two people but their lives give testimony to Christ's holiness in the church. "A good tree produces good fruit."

I'm a Catholic because, in spite of its many sinful children, the church is Christ and I believe He lives on in the world precisely in His church, which extends far beyond the world of Roman Catholicism.

How so?

The church is made up of all those who call Jesus Lord.

Why, then, are there so many warring churches if it's all supposedly one church?

Because we are sinful people. I don't like it and I know God doesn't like it, but if you concentrate on Jesus, the source of our unity, our strength and our joy, you don't worry about all that. The real problem is reaching those poor folks who don't even know Christ. If we spent all our energy criticizing one another, we'd never do anything else.

Well, let me ask another question. What does it take to prove that Jesus is God? I mean, how can you convince someone who isn't sure?

You can't prove it in a scientific way. But let's face it, there are many things we know which we can't prove in precisely that way. I go out at noon and I know the sky is filled with stars even though I can't see them. Faith in Jesus is something like that—knowing with certainty without actually seeing the proof.

Please go on. Even if you can't prove it, is there more you could say to bolster my faith?

Well let me try through a story. I know a young woman who rejects Christ. We'll call her Joan. Her parents are basically good people. She was raised in a religious home, but she gradually abandoned her faith as she passed through her teens. Now she's 25, confused, unmarried and with her second lover. One day recently her mother reproached her for the way she is living her life. Joan exploded in anger.

"Don't you dare judge me," she said. "You don't understand a thing. I don't want to bring a baby into this sick world. Your generation has given us everything but a future."

She let her mother have it; all her pent-up feelings. "Look at the world," she said, "We're going to annihilate one another. We have to live with missile silos and rocket launchers. Oil is running out, nuclear waste is increasing. One day it will poison our children. I don't want to have children depending on me when I can't even protect my own life."

She broke down in tears. After a pause, she said, "All we've got is now, mother. Don't you see that? I'm living for now, putting as much love into today as I can, because there may not be a tomorrow."

Obviously Joan is frightened, maybe even a little desperate. No one can deny that the world she's inherited is in terrible shape. You can understand her anxiety, especially anyone who is old enough to have lived through past wars and economic depressions; the threats to life in the past were just as deadly. Whether it comes by a single bullet or an all-out nuclear war, death is final. Living for the present without too much care for all the tomorrows is not a new idea. Everyone has known this temptation and lots of good people have been overwhelmed by it at one time or another. I feel sorry for Joan at this moment in her life.

How is it turning out?

She's still angry. I'd love to be able to convince her that

her resentment only makes for a joyless journey, and that there's a better way, but so far I haven't been able to. I pray for her because she's making a big mistake.

Why do you say that?

She's not happy. The illusion of happiness is never very satisfying. Obviously she thinks her present situation is the best she can do, but she can do so much better. I don't judge her. She'll learn about love and life at her own pace and in her own way. Most of us learn through the pain of trial and error. Let's just pray for her that she and others like her may find the peace of soul they're seeking.

You were starting to explain something about faith in Jesus.

Yes. I'd like to try to do it by comparing Joan to St. Augustine, the classic convert. The first half of his life was lived very much in the style of this young woman. In his autobiography, *The Confessions*, he tells his story. He lived in the fourth century in North Africa and Italy. As a young man, like youngsters of every generation, Augustine was searching. He wanted success and happiness, and he stubbornly lived life on his own terms. He had a mistress and an illegitimate child.

He was a great reader. His reading of *Hortensius* by Cicero gave him a thirst for wisdom which only intensified his search for meaning. He went from one philosophy to another, covering all the bases, including astrology. A good friend, a physician, helped Augustine work through his confusion.

Gradually his heart and mind were drawn to Christianity. He read the scriptures but at first concluded they were inferior to Cicero in style and depth. Then the moment of grace came and he wrote, "I found joy in these books, but I did not know the source of whatever was good within them." That's an interesting point by the way, he found joy in reading the scriptures.

That goes along with what you said before, about joy coming from God.

Right, he found it before he actually understood what was happening. The scales were gradually lifted from his eyes. One day he discovered Jesus Christ. Though he had heard of Christ and his mother was a devout Christian, somehow Jesus had actually escaped his notice all through his years of study. While hungering to put meaning in his life, he missed the very thing which his mother Monica had tried to teach him throughout his childhood.

Augustine wrote about his discovery of Jesus. Let me read his own words to you: "I sought for a way of gaining strength sufficient to have joy in You (God) but I did not find it until I embraced the mediator between God and man, the man Jesus Christ, who is over all things, God blessed forever."

In the next passage, Augustine quotes St. Paul. He said his dramatic moment of conversion came when he read this passage: "Not in rioting and drunkenness, not in chambering and impurities, not in strife and envying, but put you on the Lord Jesus Christ." At that moment Augustine put down the scriptures and breathed a sigh of contentment. His private rat-race was over. The struggle to find God had come to an end at last and he wrote about it:

"I had no further wish to read nor was there any need to do so. Instantly in truth...as if before a peaceful light streaming into my heart, all the dark shadows of doubt fled away."

I've never had that kind of experience.

It's a gift. Faith is a gift. That doesn't mean that God doesn't love the person who lacks faith. Augustine suffered a great deal before he found the pearl he was seeking. God is always very close to those who are searching even though they may not realize it. He's close to Joan right now. He's close to you now, whether you grasp it fully or not.

I don't know if I've answered the question. All I've done is to tell the experience of another person. But millions of Christians down through the centuries have had similar experiences and have received this gift we call faith. Once it is really accepted, life changes for us.

The miracles of Jesus, the wisdom of His teachings, the phenomenal impact He had on His times and all generations after—none of these things alone or combined can compel belief. Ultimately acceptance of Jesus is a grace. If you want to believe, keep asking and faith will be given. The very desire to believe is already a gift, one that the Lord intends to fulfill in His time and in His own way.

So even if you feel the frustration of not knowing everything as clearly as you'd like, you will in time. Take some peace in that knowledge.

I know it sounds a little like a contradiction—I say I believe and then I ask, "How do you know for sure?"

It's par for the course. Some knowledge is too much for our comprehension, it simply staggers the imagination. For instance, even though we believe in a place called "heaven," we can't picture it because we've never been there. And if you can't picture something, you don't feel as though you really know it. So faith in a certain sense is incomplete knowledge—"a seeing in darkness." Only

when we see God "face to face" will we really know the
fullness of truth. Do you mind if I tell you a little story?

No, please do.

The meaning of heaven came home to me a few years
ago through the life of a friend whom I shall call Beatrice.
When I first met her she was in her early 40s. She was
totally paralyzed from the neck down. For 17 years she lay
in bed, imprisoned in her own body and cared for by a
loving mother. Polio had destroyed her mobility. Her
husband eventually deserted her. There were no children.

Understandably, she was full of resentment and resisted all my efforts to be cheerful. But we prayed together
and with God's help there was slow progress.

Almost from the beginning I found myself talking to
her about heaven. There was little else I could do. We began planning future picnics in heaven, excursions to some
idyllic beach. She liked it. I promised one day I would es-
cort her to a marvelous heavenly feast, and we would
laugh and sing in the company of angels and saints. Caged
in her limp body, her spirit brightened.

I helped her to picture what heaven might be like. I
don't know any more about it than you do, but I believe
we will be supremely happy with God forever.

I helped Beatrice, but she helped me even more.
Through her I came to understand more clearly the spiritual truths expressed in the Beatitudes.

They clearly emphasize the eschatological motivation
of the ethics of the gospel. It's not that those mentioned—
the poor, the meek, those who suffer persecution, etc.—
are already happy within themselves as the world knows
happiness, but they are promised eternal happiness and
they know their fate is going to be wonderful in the future
world. Jesus pronounces this judgment of God to console

them and enable them to prepare interiorly to bear their immediate cross with joy and peaceful resignation. Precisely when they do that, they experience mystical joy. It fills them with courage and, yes, even a kind of euphoria.

If Jesus were to speak to Beatrice, I think He'd say:

"Beatrice, be happy, your body may be useless now, but you have a whole eternity for health and vitality.

"Beatrice, be happy, you suffer much now, but soon you will be filled with an inexpressible glory.

"Beatrice, be happy, you are paralyzed now, but the time is coming when you will dance forever in the light of God's love."

In Beatrice's 18th year of confinement, her mother died. Shortly after she was put in a home. She never recovered from the shock. She died peacefully in her sleep a few weeks later. Love had kept her alive all those years and it was love that finally brought her home.

Knowing well that the Lord keeps all His promises, I am happy for Beatrice. For Beatrice and for each one of us, the resurrection of Jesus means love and full life, forever. Ultimately, the secret of Christian joy is rooted in Jesus Christ and His resurrection.

One Solitary Life

He was born in an obscure village
the child of a peasant woman.
He grew up in still another village,
where he worked in a carpenter shop
until he was thirty.
Then for three years
he was an itinerant preacher.
He never wrote a book.
He never held an office.
He never had a family or owned a house.

He didn't go to college.
He never visited a big city.
He never traveled two hundred miles
    from the place where he was born.
He did none of the things
    one usually associates with greatness.
He had no credentials but himself.
He was only thirty-three
    when the tide of public opinion
    turned against him.
His friends ran away.
He was turned over to his enemies
    and went through the mockery of a trial.
He was nailed to a cross
    between two thieves.
While he was dying,
    his executioners gambled for his clothing,
    the only property he had on earth.
When he was dead,
    he was laid in a borrowed grave
    through the pity of a friend.
Nineteen centuries have come and gone,
    and today he is the central figure
    of the human race,
    and the leader of mankind's progress.
All the armies that ever marched,
    all the navies that ever sailed,
    all the parliaments that ever sat,
    all the kings that ever reigned,
    put together,
    have not affected
    the life of man on earth
    as much as that One Solitary Life.

Anonymous

CHAPTER TWO

The Words of Jesus

Enter into the joy of thy Lord.

(Mt. 25:21)

This invitation of Jesus is extended to you with no pressure and no strings. You're free to seek the wellsprings of joy in God, or not, as you like.

At the birth of Christ the angels sang: "... Good tidings of great joy." (Lk. 2:10) He was the fulfillment of our ancient longings. But even before Christ, it was understood that union with God brings joy. "In Thy presence is fullness of joy." (Ps. 16:11) David, at a dark time in his life, wrote these words, "Restore unto me the joy of Thy salvation" (Ps. 51:12) because he understood that God is the fountain of joy.

Since the birth of Jesus this knowledge about our destiny has become more refined. We know spiritual joy is not a passing emotion, it is not mere sentiment. It is an attitude of life, intimately related with the presence and the person of Jesus Christ.

Let's explore together the mystery of joy in Jesus, for He is the Supreme Revelation of God.

* * *

Everyone, then, who hears these words of Mine and acts upon them I will compare him to a wise man who built his house on rock—and the rain fell, and the torrents came, and the winds blew and battered that house, but it did not fall, because it was founded on rock; while everyone who hears these words of Mine and does not act upon them will be like a foolish man who built his house on sand—and the rain fell, and the torrents came, and the winds blew and battered that house, and it fell, and mighty was its fall!

(Mt. 7:24–27)

The words Jesus spoke when He lived and worked 2,000 years ago are all about joy. Powerful in their time, they continue to have a vital impact on people today. For me, five words capture the essence of His message: love, forgive, pray, go, teach.

Jesus asks us to act upon His words, and we know we can because, with God's help, everything is possible. The trick is getting yourself in a frame of mind where you can truly enter into His life.

A life rooted in God is one filled with His reality. It's a life where God's Spirit does the leading. In such a state of surrender we might find ourselves drawn to a place we never fancied for ourselves.

Our faith, then, is more than words. Our faith is a kind of joyful surrender. In dying on the cross, Jesus did more than believe in God the Father. He obeyed. He went to Jerusalem against the advice of friends because God asked it. He knew the danger before Him, but He went anyway.

Love

While we may not be asked to die on a cross, we may be prompted by the Holy Spirit to die to one way of living in favor of another. If you're interested in joy, you'll want to learn more about selfless love—the kind of love revealed in this story about a boy who wanted to be a singer, but whose teacher gave him little hope, telling him, "You sound like the wind in the shutters!"

His mother believed in him, however. She sent him to another teacher. To pay for her son's lessons she went without shoes, sometimes even without food.

The boy was Enrico Caruso. He became the greatest tenor of his time—because a mother loved him and had faith in him.

Jesus spoke often about love:

Love the Lord your God with all your heart and with all your soul and with all your intelligence. This is the great and first commandment. And the second is similar to it: You shall love your neighbor as yourself. On these two commandments depend all the law and the prophets.

(Mt. 22:37–40)

As the Father loved Me, so I loved you: abide in My love. If you keep My commandments, you will abide in My love, as I have kept My Father's command and abide in Him.

(Jn. 15:9–10)

Greater love no man has than to lay down his life for his friends.

(Jn. 15:13)

The word "love" comes from the Latin word "delegere," meaning "to choose," and choice always implies the renunciation of other possible options. To choose a spouse is to turn from others. To lay down your life for your friends is to give up your own life, the supreme act of love. Love involves choices all along the way.

A servant of God does not live a life tightly coiled around his or her own pleasures or interests. Love is a higher calling. We know that we will all be judged on love; not so much on what we did as on how much love we put into the doing. Sometimes love will lead us to be gentle:

Come, blessed ones of My Father: inherit the kingdom prepared for you. . . for I was hungry and you gave Me to eat, I was thirsty and you gave Me to drink, I was a stranger and you took Me in. . . anything you did to one of the least of these My brothers, you did to Me.

(Mt. 25:34, 35, 40)

Sometimes love will be expressed in strong language, with clear demands:

Unless you take up your cross you are not worthy of Me.

(Mt. 10:38)

Forgive

Love and forgiveness are intimately related. We hurt one another so often, it takes great love to mend the fences and heal the wounds.

Forgiveness is a gentle form of love. Forgiveness is also a precondition of prayer. Here's a story which speaks eloquently of the beauty of a forgiving heart.

Clara Barton, founder of the American nursing profession, never held a grudge. Once a friend reminded her of something cruel that had been done to her but she seemed not to remember it.

"Don't you remember the wrong that was done to you?" the friend asked. "No," Clara answered, "I distinctly remember forgetting that."

If, then, you bring your gift to the altar, and there remember your brother has something against you, leave your gift before the altar: go first and be reconciled with your brother, and then come back and offer your gift.

(Mt. 5:23–24)

And whenever you stand praying, forgive, if you have anything against any one; so that your Father also who is in heaven may forgive you your trespasses.

(Mk. 11:25)

Pray

Once we are free enough to forgive, we are free enough to pray.

A bible which Abraham Lincoln often used as President falls open easily to Psalm 34. There is a smudge at one spot where the President apparently rested his fingers and meditated. The verse reads: "I sought the Lord, and He answered me and delivered me from all my fears."

Jesus inspired us to pray:

Ask, and it shall be given to you; seek, and you shall find; knock, and it shall be opened to you. For everyone who asks receives, and he who seeks finds, and to him who knocks it shall be opened.

(Mt. 7:7–8)

And when you pray, be not like the hypocrites who love to stand. . .so people will see them. Indeed, I tell you, they have received their reward. When you pray, go into your room, close your door, and pray to your Father in

secret, and your Father, who penetrates secrets, will re-
ward you openly.

Now, while you pray, don't prattle as do the pagans
who believe they will be heard because of their many
words. Don't imitate them, for your Father knows what
you need even before you ask Him. Instead, pray like this:

> *Our Father who art in heaven,*
>   *hallowed be Thy name.*
> *Thy kingdom come, Thy will be done*
>   *on earth as it is in heaven.*
> *Give us this day our daily bread,*
>   *and forgive us our trespasses*
>   *as we forgive those who trespass against us.*
> *And lead us not into temptation*
>   *but deliver us from the evil one.*

(Mt. 6:5–13)

Go

Prayer gives us the power to bear good fruit, the power
to go about the task of establishing His kingdom of truth,
justice, peace and grace.

I remember reading about a disabled woman who
prayed often and well. The Lord showed her a way to express her love in spite of her handicap. From her home in
Cannington, Canada, Dorthea Monteith learned to spread
friendship and encouragement to thousands of lonely
shut-ins even though she herself has been confined to a
wheelchair for years.

Each day she spends several hours mailing a newsletter,
poetry and encouraging notes to aged and handicapped
people she has never met. She obtains their names and ad-
dresses from magazines for shut-ins and from friends
who write or visit. Often she includes some small item
such as a bookmark or tea bag.

Of her own troubles, she says nothing. "I feel the Lord has permitted me to be a shut-in for His glory," she says. Dorthea listened to the words of Jesus. She found joy in spite of her troubles. Her life is a response to the command to "go":

Go and learn what this means: "I desire mercy, and not sacrifice." I have come to call sinners, not the just.

(Mt. 9:13)

Go along the valleys and the paths; force the people to come in, so that My house may be full.

(Lk. 14:23)

Go and seek what has gone astray.

(Mt. 18:12)

Go into the whole world and preach the gospel to every creature.

(Mk. 16:15)

Go and sin no more.

(Jn. 8:11)

The Spirit leads us in different ways through the words of Jesus. He challenges us to strive for supernatural goals, not merely human ones. He offers His support:

Let not your hearts be troubled, believe in God and believe in Me. In My Father's house, there are many mansions, otherwise would I have told you that I was going to prepare a place for you? And when I will have gone and prepared a place for you, I will come back and take you with Me, so that you can be where I am. And you know where I am going, and you know the way.

(Jn. 14:1–4)

Some words of Jesus often cited in our own Christopher literature are these:

You are the light of the world. A city on top of a hill cannot be hidden, nor do men light a lamp to place it under a basket: they set it on a stand where it shines upon all in the house. Likewise, let your light shine forth upon men so that they may notice your good deeds and give glory to your Father in Heaven.

(Mt. 5:14–16)

We believe there is great joy in allowing the Lord to shine in us. God wants us to put His words into practice. Our good deeds not only teach others, they give forth a light that glorifies the Father.

Teach

A believer and a skeptic went for a walk. The skeptic said, "Look at the trouble and misery in the world after thousands of years of religion. What good is religion?

His companion noticed a child, filthy with grime, playing in the gutter. He said, "We've had soap for generation after generation yet look how dirty that child is. Of what value is soap?"

The skeptic protested, "But soap can't do any good unless it is used!"

"Exactly," replied the believer.

Teaching others how to live the Christian life is part of our calling:

Go and teach all the peoples, everywhere baptizing them in the name of the Father and of the Son and of the Holy Spirit, teach them to obey all the commands I have given you; and remember I will be with you until the end of time.

(Mt. 28:19–20)

A good teacher is one who lives the life. But sometimes our goodness causes a negative reaction in others. If that happens, Jesus has some advice:

. . . Don't worry about how you will answer or what you will say: for at that hour, the Holy Spirit will teach you what to say.

(Lk. 12:11-12)

Think about Jesus as the supreme revelation of God. To know Him is to know the mind of God. His advice is sound and trustworthy:

Whoever sees Me sees the One who sent Me. I have come as light to the world, so no one who believes in Me is left in the dark.

(Jn. 12:45-46)

I am the true vine, and My Father is the vine-tender. Every barren twig in Me, He prunes, and every fruitful one He trims to increase its yield. Now, you are already pure because of the words I have spoken to you. . . remain in Me as I will in you. As a branch cannot bear fruit on its own, but must remain on the vine, neither can you unless you abide in Me. I am the vine, you are the branches. He who abides in Me, and I in him, he is the one who bears much fruit; for without Me you can do nothing.

(Jn. 15:1-5)

* * *

Love, forgive, pray, go, teach. These words of Jesus contain the essence of His message and the secret of our joy. Jesus teaches us that God loved us first, He created us for a particular purpose in life. Each one of us has a job to do that nobody else in the world can do; and when we find that mission, we will be in harmony with our Maker. All spiritual joy is related to the way we respond to the words of Jesus. He teaches us God's supreme law of love. One text sums it up perfectly:

> *You did not choose Me: I chose you and established you, that you may go and bring forth fruit. And your fruit will last, so that whatever you ask the Father in My name will be granted . . . love one another.*
>
> (Jn. 15:16–17)

To be joyful is to be a carrier of divine love.

CHAPTER THREE

Love

Each person's mission is a mission of love. But you must have time for your own first, and after that you can work for others. Begin in the place where you are, with the people closest to you. Make your homes centers of compassion and forgive endlessly. Let no one ever come to you without coming away better and happier.

Mother Teresa

Mother Teresa of Calcutta, the Nobel Prize winner, is a favorite of mine. She is truly a Christbearer, a carrier of Divine Love. We've all heard the saying "Charity begins at home" a thousand times. Well it does. But what does that mean?

Love is a word that has been devalued by overuse. Love takes energy and determination. Why? Because it's so difficult to enter into the pain of another. We recoil from the burdens of love. It takes strength to go back and give when you feel like running away.

Growing in one's ability to love is an art and a skill that is first learned at home. Some never learn it because it's not taught at home. But when it's done well we can be tender and—when appropriate—tough. Sometimes youngsters must be told that we demand honesty of them, courtesy, and all the social virtues that make living tolerable. Love can be very stern.

Ultimately, success in communicating love is a matter of openness to God's Spirit. Those who love best learn how to make God's strength and joy their own. It's at home that we learn our limits, that we learn to take care of first things first.

Believing in God's love is the greatest stimulant to human love. Let me tell you about a young woman who learned this the hard way.

She had been blessed with three beautiful children in less than two-and-a-half years. The second delivery brought twins, a boy and a girl.

Ann (I've changed her name) had hardly gotten used to motherhood when she had three babies to manage. She admitted that she was a bit lazy as a teenager. Ann loved her sleep in those days and boasted of needing nine hours a night just to function. After her first child she was exhausted. The demands of her infant seemed overwhelming; she dreamed of escaping, perhaps by way of a part-time job. Ann loved her tiny son but at the same time resented the absolute demands he made upon her. In a short time she was shocked to find herself pregnant again.

After the twins arrived, she was again on the verge of collapse and thought of running away. But she prayed for the strength to hang on and do her job. The Lord heard her prayer, and Ann's life was turned around.

When I met her she was bubbling with joy, bragging how each of the children would play for awhile and then run over to give her a hug and run off. They needed the occasional reassurance of her presence. It made her feel needed and happy.

"I'm glad now I had the twins," she said. "I find it easier with the three than it was when I had only one."

The truth is it's probably three times as much work, but Ann learned to accept her life in a new way. Even though she is now averaging only five hours sleep a night, she's happy. The old ways of doing exactly what she wanted, when she wanted, are a thing of the past. She has grown up. In praying for the grace to meet the challenge of love, she found peace and a heightened sense of self-respect; both ingredients of a joyful life. In addition, she is constantly bolstered by the love she gets back from her children and her husband. Love begets love.

All of this reminds me of the words of the wedding ceremony: "Marriage can be difficult and irksome at times, but love can make it easy, and perfect love can make it a joy." The connection between joy and love is again evident.

Families are individuals joined by blood or marriage, trying to love one another. The constant effort of love always involves a give and take. At times some members of the family have greater needs than others: age, physical or mental health, economic state, level of maturity, all these things have a bearing on family strain. Some people are more difficult to live with than others, but all behavior is derived from need. People need people and the best place —for some, the only place—to meet most of those needs is in the family setting.

It helps to come together from time to time to share feelings and problems, to awaken a family spirit of solidarity and support.

Family Rap Sessions

One of the best ideas I've come across in a long time is the practice of "family night." Traditionally the Mormons set aside Monday nights for family activities. The same model has been adopted by many other church groups.

The results are encouraging, particularly in the area of communication. These get-togethers aim at creating an atmosphere of emotional comfort for each person in the family. When feelings are ventilated people feel better.

Some even plan family goals at their meetings. One family decided they could do without television one day a week. As a result, each member found more time for other worthwhile projects. In some rap sessions it became clear that the mother was being taken too much for granted. The rest of the family decided to shoulder some of her responsibilities around the house. Mom was a lot happier, because it was done as a gesture of love.

One man rejected a promotion after talking it out with the family because he felt the move would take him away from home too much. The children expressed a need for more attention and he listened. All concerned felt better.

A family discussion led the Donald Kramer family of Brooklyn Center, Minnesota, to give Mrs. Kramer's brother-in-law and his wife a weekend away from the farm. The idea was to give them a chance to catch their breath. So Donald Kramer and his wife and children moved in for a weekend. They took care of the children at the farm and milked the farm's 40 cows. A great sacrifice for them, no doubt, but it was so warmly appreciated they were all happier because of having done it.

"Charity begins at home" but it also reaches out to others. The whole family can cooperate in all kinds of love projects once everyone agrees. It takes planning and time, but it's worth it.

Take a look at your own family situation. Perhaps something like a "family night" would be welcomed by everybody and provide some memorable experiences. If you don't think it would be accepted by the others don't give up. Convince just one person in the family and the two of you can work on the others one by one. You'll be amazed at how much you can accomplish with teamwork.

Lots of people find ways of reaching out to others.

A Mother to 84 Youngsters

Letters come to the Christopher office by the hundreds every day. One in particular I want to share with you came from Dorathea M. Koons of Troy, Ohio. She wrote:

"I am an ordinary person doing what God has called me to do. I care for little ones who need someone to love them. So far the county has given me 84."

Eighty-four children! It seemed impossible, so I called Mrs. Koons to find out more. It was a delightful conversation. She has been a foster mother for Miami County in Ohio since 1966. When her second husband died of cancer in 1974, she thought they would declare her ineligible as a foster parent, but her fears were unwarranted. They gave her another child right away.

"I was a widow, but that wasn't going to stop me from doing what I wanted to do," she said. I asked her about the finances involved. "The county gives clothes, medicine and $3 a day for each child," she told me, "but I supply everything else."

"Everything else," it turns out, includes a special brand of tender love. In fact, county authorities go out of their way to bring her the sick children because of her special gifts. Pam Severs, supervisor of foster care for Miami County Children's Services, says "Dorathea has the amazing capacity to deal with sick children, and she's particularly good with infants."

"How did you come by this gift," I asked Mrs. Koons.

"I do it out of love. I could never have children of my own," she said. "After a miscarriage in 1933 I was told I would never have a child, but since then I have been a mother to over 150 children of all ages." She began in 1933 taking care of neighborhood children whose parents temporarily couldn't manage.

"I just did it for love of the children," she said. "Those were the Depression days and people were suffering terribly. It was the joy of that experience that led me to begin serving the county program. God has been good to me."

She added: "I just love children. I just love them—what can I say!"

Dorathea Koons doesn't have to say anything. Her actions say it all, and she touches more than the lives of her little children. She is showing all of us what one person can do in the lives of others. We are never too old or too young to give love.

* * *

I think fathers and mothers have an added burden these days because of the mood of our times. There's an incipient kind of selfishness promoted in the modern world. It takes a special effort to inspire children to be givers and not takers. It takes prayer and grace.

In the 1960s the in-phrase was "do your own thing." It was self-oriented but it allowed for some altruism and a certain individuality of style in expressing one's idealism. Doing your own thing could, after all, be interpreted as finding "fulfillment" by serving others.

In the 70s we seemed to swing back to the 19th-century Darwinian individualism, "the survival of the fittest." Reaching out to help others was actually considered dumb. Robert Ringer, a popular self-help writer, wrote, "Concentrate on looking out for Number One; I'm sure you have enough problems of your own without worrying about helping others."

To concentrate only on yourself is natural and understandable but it is also spiritually immature. Seeking one's own satisfaction first and always without regard for others is the guarantee of an empty future because it is the denial of love. The law of love is as ancient as the human race. Thousands of years before Christ was born, the golden rule was extolled on planet Earth. For instance, Yoga, an ancient Hindu discipline going back far beyond recorded history, is based on the idea that there are two paths to follow in life: The Path of Desire or the Path of Renunciation.

The Path of Desire begins with man's craving for pleasure. The Hindu says pleasure is good, but eventually it becomes stale and unsatisfying because it is too self-absorbed. Higher than the pleasure-seeking principle is the pursuit of worldly success. But since worldly success centers on self, it too is considered by the Hindus to be limited and temporary.

As the Hindu grows in maturity, he or she is taught to realize that the Path of Desire does not bring happiness. So they turn willingly to the Path of Renunciation.

The Path of Renunciation begins with service. Service to neighbor is considered a superior way of life, and much more satisfying. But, because it is finite in its goal, the real answer is found only in God. Ultimate happiness comes when one ascends to true Union, the most advanced degree of the Path of Renunciation. It implies an opening up to God in contemplation, a surrender of self to His Holy Presence.

Jesus, who is the Way, said, "You shall love the Lord your God with all your heart, and with all your soul, and with all your mind . . . and you shall love your neighbor as yourself." (Mt. 22:37–39) He also said, "If you love those who love you, what thanks can you expect? Even sinners love those who love them." (Lk. 6:31–32)

Jesus wants our joy to be full, and it will be if we learn to love.

I was struck by a dialogue homily one morning when I

was visiting a community of Benedictine monks. One of the Brothers spoke of the need for discipline in the Christian's life. He read from the Rule of Taize, written by Brother Roger Shutz, the founder and the prior of an ecumenical monastic community in Taize, France.

> . . . Do not impose discipline on yourself for its own sake. Gaining mastery of yourself has no aim other than to render you more available. Let there be no useless asceticism; hold only to the works God commands. Carry the burdens of others, accept the petty injuries of each day, so as to share concretely in the sufferings of Christ . . . this is our first discipline . . . Be a sign of joy and love among men.

How beautiful . . . "Be a sign of joy and love among men . . ." "Let there be no useless asceticism." I learned a lot from this visit.

Many religious people follow elaborate rules to become holy. These are good insofar as they foster the love of God, but very often they become an end in themselves. In this interpretation we see that the aim of self-discipline is to "render yourself more available." St. Paul says, "Help carry the burdens of others, in this way you will fulfill the law of Jesus Christ." (Gal. 6:2)

Jesus is often perceived as a strict disciplinarian who limits and constricts our freedom. In reality He is the One who liberates us fully. St. Benedict, a true follower of Jesus, was also a liberator. In 1980 we celebrated the 1500th anniversary of his monastic way of life. The vows of poverty, chastity and obedience, the basis of Benedictine spirituality, are in actuality three great freedoms. Those who take such vows shake themselves free of excess baggage. If lived properly, poverty of spirit gives us freedom from materialism; the spirit of chastity liberates us from sexual preoccupation; and the vow of obedience is designed to release us from the tyranny of egoism and self-will. All of this is done to free oneself to love, to be more available to others.

Christian ascetism, when properly lived, renders a person more open to a life of loving service. The more you get outside of yourself, the freer you become.

* * *

If I can do some good today,
If I can serve along life's way,
If I can something helpful say,
  Lord, show me how.

If I can right a human wrong,
If I can help to make one strong,
If I can cheer with smile or song,
  Lord, show me how.

If I can aid one in distress,
If I can make a burden less,
If I can spread more happiness,
  Lord, show me how.

To laugh often and much:
To win the respect of intelligent people
  and the affection of children,
To earn the appreciation of honest critics
  and endure the betrayal of false friends;
To appreciate beauty,
To find the best in others,
To leave the world a bit better,
  whether by a healthy child, a garden patch
  or a redeemed social condition;
To know even one life has
breathed easier because you lived,
  This is to have succeeded.

Ralph Waldo Emerson

CHAPTER FOUR

Forgive

Jesus makes an important point again and again:

If, then, you bring your gift to the altar, and there remember your brother has something against you, leave your gift before the altar; go first and be reconciled with your brother, and then come back and offer your gift.

(Mt. 5:23-24)

The spirit of forgiveness is a key element in our pursuit of happiness. To live well it is necessary to strive for a forgiving heart. "Forgive us our trespasses as we forgive those who trespass against us." If only it were easy to do. It isn't.

A priest friend of mine was mugged and stabbed by a drug addict. For 15 years he served his people in a black parish in Jersey City, New Jersey.

He was well loved by his people but the neighborhood had its share of drug addicts and drifters. It was a drifter who attacked him one night as he walked from his garage to the rectory. The robber got away with his wallet but not before the priest was knifed in his side, his shoulder and his face.

Two months later we had dinner together and he told me that he had forgiven the assailant a thousand times. "I pray for him," he said, "but I'm furious. I can't seem to turn off the anger. I find myself fighting with him in my dreams."

Before I comment on this reaction, permit me to tell you one more story. This one is about a young woman in her late 20s. Her parents divorced after raising a large family. All through her childhood she felt she was in the middle of a fight. Her father was both alcoholic and irresponsible as a provider and a parent.

After the divorce she forgave him everything and prayed for him. Then he married a much younger woman and overcame his drinking problem. The daughter became jealous and resentful of his new wife. She resented being deprived of his love and affection all those years, she was angry that a complete stranger, her own age, was receiving the love that she felt rightfully belonged to her and her mother.

She forgave him, yes, a thousand times over; she even prayed for him. But the anger wouldn't go away.

There are many variations on this theme of victimization. Injustice is always wrong. Innocence should never have to suffer at the hands of the unjust but it happens, over and over again, and the wounds are always deep. The scars of anger do not vanish overnight. Jesus, the perfectly innocent one, was condemned at an unjust trial and nailed to a cross. When He rose from the dead the scars on His hands and His side were still clearly visible.

Jesus, the Holy of Holies, offered all His sufferings and humiliations in a spirit of reparation, but the scars were still on His hands.

Deep and ugly are the emotional scars inflicted by those who cause us pain. Even that good priest, who truly forgave his attacker, couldn't discard the immediate after-effect of his pain and fury. All his human instincts of self-preservation had been intensely activated. Whereas before he was relatively confident and secure in his parish, now, like a wounded animal, he became alert to danger, defensive, ready to fight for his life. These are all instincts God put in us. It will take time for his nervous system to return to normal. But his heart is a forgiving heart. He'll make it.

The Lord sees all our good intentions. When we are united with the heart of Christ, the healing is well under way. My point is this: negative feelings do not cancel the authenticity of our forgiveness. Forgiveness is a thing apart from the anxiety, the guilt and the fear we may experience for a long time after we've been hurt. To decide to forgive is to forgive. Both the priest and the young woman prayed to forgive totally. Their feelings lagged behind. In time complete peace will come, but for the present each of them will have to be content with the humiliation of mixed feelings.

There are two stages of Christian forgiveness. The first is forgiveness itself, the second is thanksgiving. Nothing erases the hurts of the past faster than a grateful heart. In the total picture we have so much for which to be grateful. When we concentrate on the good things of life, our hurts become insignificant. In terms of eternity, all trouble is a passing moment.

In the spirit of thanksgiving it's possible to face someone who has hurt you and truly wish them peace, happiness, good health and eternal salvation—even if you still feel some revulsion for that person. The forgiveness is real, the feelings have not yet caught up. It's human to be mixed up. We're little. In our feeble attempts at dispensing divine mercy, we often fall short of God's perfection. It's soothing to know that when God forgives, He forgives totally, perfectly, without hesitation. But we humans are not God.

Even the saints had trouble along these lines. For instance, St. Therese, the Little Flower, had bad feelings toward one of her religious sisters. She knew she could not love her as Jesus asked: "Love one another as I have loved you." As often as she tried, she could not.

Then she received a great grace. Therese realized that an act which might be impossible for her was always possible for the Lord who abided in her. So she turned to Him in a moment of grace and said, "I myself cannot love this sister as You love her, Lord, but *You*, living in me, can love her for me and through me." She simply turned over the problem to Jesus and relaxed. She ignored her inadequate feelings. They were irrelevant. She trusted Jesus to supply the perfect love and perfect forgiveness called for in the gospel.

When Therese died, the sister who was once the object of her revulsion said, "I believe I was her favorite, Therese always had a special affection for me."

The Lord has His own way of working through our imperfections when we turn to Him in faith.

* * *

In her book, *Something More*, Catherine Marshall writes about a time when she and her husband had problems that seemed to resist their prayers; they decided to act literally on Jesus' words, "And when you stand in prayer, forgive whatever you have against anybody."

So each day they spent time putting on paper any grievances they had against anybody. They read them aloud, forgave the persons involved, then destroyed the papers.

It was like a cleansing for each of them, a lovely spiritual practice.

Why do so many people devoted to Christ miss the importance of a forgiving heart? Would we have so much division among Christians if our forgiveness was greater?

If you have a flood in the basement, it is far wiser to turn off the water before you begin bailing out. The same with prayer. Lots of good people pray and pray but they feel justified and self-righteous about their grudges. If you've been abused by someone, only you can understand how much it hurts, but the Lord asks you to forgive, even if forgiveness offends your sense of justice. He asks it, and we, if we are serious about our faith and our prayer, should be wise enough to obey. If we do, our lives will be enriched, our prayer will be more abundantly fruitful, our peace will be restored, and our joy will be deepened.

What, then, is forgiveness? Forgiveness has to do with a "giving" before you feel like "giving." It's not logical or comfortable I know, but it is what the Spirit asks of us.

Forgiveness is showing mercy even when the injury has been deliberate. It's easy to forgive when we can find an excuse for what was done, but forgiving when there is none, that's tough. But that's when forgiveness is most needed. Jesus didn't deny the sin of the woman about to be stoned for adultery. He showed mercy. Mercy is the attitude of love toward misery. He told her, "Go and sin no more," but He never withheld His forgiveness.

When you forgive you accept the person as he or she is. It is accepting the unruly child, the disloyal friend, the overbearing mother. It is letting go of judgments. People can learn to deepen relationships once they forgive one another for not being equal to their expectations. This has to be done over and over. When you forgive you take a

risk, you become vulnerable. Some might call it foolishness, because renewing a commitment to the friend who
has betrayed trust could lead to being hurt again. Jesus
taught that the risk is worth it.

Forgiveness is accepting an apology. It is graciously re-
specting the effort of reconciliation, even when the hurt is
deep or when it is not.

I know a woman who worked herself up to make a difficult apology; she got an abrupt response, "Forget it. It
wasn't important." She felt terribly let down. To her, it
was important and she needed to be forgiven.

If you get the knack of it, *forgiveness can be a way of
living.* Developing a readiness to forgive is important. By
pardoning others for the little everyday hurts and annoy-
ances; by pardoning ourselves for small things, too, we
grow in grace; we develop a forgiving heart. Living this
way prepares us to handle the more important injuries
and blunders.

James G. T. Fairfield, author of *When You Don't
Agree*, sees forgiveness as the first skill of self-giving love.
"It takes the hurt," he says, "acknowledges the problem,
accepts the person and loves in the direction of resolving
the situation."

When I am the offender, God does this for me. The
other person may or may not forgive me. But when I accept God's forgiveness, I am choosing to forgive—and
love—myself. Sometimes we have to learn to forgive ourselves before we can forgive others. By that I mean we truly
have to accept God's love here and now.

Forgiveness is not sentimental, not condescending, not
righteous. Above all, it is not conditional. God's love is
pure. Our love is not. Sometimes we are like petulant children. It's childish, for instance, to stand on ceremony,
saying: "I'll forgive you if you'll apologize."

Jesus told the story of the prodigal son who went off and wasted his inheritance in debauchery. When he returned, devastated and chastened, he was prepared to bargain with his father by becoming a hired servant.

But the father didn't even let him begin. He hurried to meet him, kissed him, ordered robes to be brought, a feast to be prepared. No ifs or buts. "I'll take you in if you promise never to do it again."

The father loves and forgives without bargaining, without conditions. So too God the Father accepts us as we are. This is what He asks us to do for one another.

* * *

A spirit of forgiveness is the first step toward joy.

Prophetic religion through the ages has stressed the need for forgiveness and tolerance... psychology now supplements this insight by teaching us that we can achieve inner health only through forgiveness—the forgiveness not only of others but also of ourselves...

Joshua Liebman

A woman wrote to columnist Ann Landers to thank her for a column published eight years before: "It was the 'forgive and forget' answer you gave to a woman with small children and a husband with a 'wandering eye.' You said... 'Don't be stubborn or proud. Take him back. I promise you won't regret it'."

The letter writer was in such a situation herself when she read the column. She felt unable to forgive but she took the advice because it seemed meant for her. "The eight years that followed were our happiest," she wrote, noting that her husband had recently died. "The warmth of the memories of our last years together will sustain me forever," she added.

Forgiveness bears good fruit, and certainly banishes resentment, the enemy of joy.

When the burdens of resentment and guilt are dropped, things begin to happen—both to the forgiver and the forgiven. It's like opening a dam and letting the water flow. Power is released.

I know when I forgive and when I accept forgiveness I feel whole: healed of conflict and free to love myself and others. The theologian Martin Marty agrees: "Forgiving and being forgiven are experiences that allow me to be free for a new day."

All of us have difficulties with forgiveness; difficulties with asking for forgiveness, accepting it when it is offered —even with forgiving ourselves.

There are no formulas, no easy answers, but here are a few suggestions.

■ Try looking squarely at the injury you have done or that has been done to you. Acknowledge your feeling of guilt or resentment. Without forgiveness, this feeling will deepen and harden. Ask yourself if you want to live with that kind of burden.

■ Do something. Take some action as soon as possible: a letter, a word, a kindness, a hug, an apology, a prayer. To forgive is to decide something. Express that decision.

■ Ask yourself, "What pressures was that person feeling?" Or, "What would I have done in those circumstances?" Some injuries are unintended or unavoidable. Maybe there's good reason to forgive.

■ Remember the words of Jesus when Peter asked, "'Lord, how many times must I forgive my brother if he wrongs me. As often as seven times?' 'No,' said

Jesus, 'Not seven times; I say, seventy times seven times'." (Mt. 19:22)

■ Fight the fears within you. Forgiveness is total or it is nothing. It is a risk and risk is seldom easy. Feeling threatened is natural in these cases. It is the price of love.

■ Think about being forgiven for the greatest wrong you have ever done. Doesn't that feel great? It is in your power to give this gift to someone else. Forgiveness is a precious gift. Why not give it? So what if it's not appreciated. You'll be the bigger person. You'll be doing the Lord's will.

■ Pray for the grace to say, "I'm sorry," if you're the one who needs to be forgiven. God will answer that prayer. What if you feel you don't deserve forgiveness? Who does? God our Father is extravagant with His forgiveness. He asks us to be the same: toward ourselves, to everybody, for everything. Instantly. Continually. With God all things are possible.

Dealing With Your Feelings

Once the decision to forgive is made the rest is in God's hands. Healing will come at its own pace.

Before Jesus said to the paralytic, "Take up your bed and walk," He said, "Take heart, son, your sins are forgiven." (Mt. 9:2, 6) Healing and forgiveness are continually combined in the gospels.

We are paralyzed until we accept—really accept—the fact that God forgives us. Once we do, we are freed to love, forgive and accept ourselves. Then the joy of healing begins.

When a Nazi concentration camp was liberated, this prayer by a Jewish prisoner was found on a scrap of paper:

*Peace be to men of bad will, and an end to all revenge
    and to all words of pain and punishment. . .
So many have borne witness with their blood!
O God, do not put their suffering upon the scales of
    Thy justice,
Lest it be counted to the hangman, lest he be brought to
    answer for his atrocities.
But to all hangmen and informers, to all traitors and
    evil ones, do grant the benefit of the courage and
    fortitude shown by those others, who were their
    victims. . .
Grant the benefit of the burning love and sacrifice in
    those harrowed, tortured hearts, which remained
    strong and steadfast in the face of death and unto
    their weakest hour.
All this, O Lord, may it count in Thine eyes, so that
    their sins be forgiven.
May this be the ransom that restores justice.
And all that is good, let it be counted, and all that is evil,
    let it be wiped out. . .
May peace come once more upon this earth, peace to
    men of good will; and may it descend upon the others
    also. Amen.*

                        From Dimanche, a French weekly.

Returning good for evil is at the heart of the gospel; forgiveness is the sine qua non of holiness. Once you say, "I
forgive":

■ Believe that you have truly forgiven.

■ Accept all the negative emotions as a temporary an-
noyance. Offer the anger, the hurt you feel in union
with Christ's offering on the cross, in reparation for
your sins and for the sins of the whole world.

■ Cultivate a grateful heart by continually thanking God.

In all circumstances give thanks to the Lord, for this is the will of God for you.

(1 Thess. 5:18)

* * *

All my life I have noticed that outstanding people of every religion have something very special in common. They all possess the fundamental wisdom that we are children of a gracious God, a God who loves us dearly, and they are grateful. Their gratitude makes for sweetness of spirit.

God is unchanging love. And our best response to honor His love is gratitude. Listen to the voices of some leading religious thinkers:

Helen Keller: "For three things I thank God every day of my life: Thanks that He has vouchsafed me knowledge of His works; deep thanks that He has set in my darkness the lamp of faith; deep, deepest thanks that I have another life to look forward to—a joyous life with light, flowers and heavenly song."

Dietrich Bonhoeffer: "I am sure of God's hand and guidance...I am thankful to go the way which I am being led. My past life is full of God's mercy, and above all sin stands the forgiving love of the crucified."

Martin Buber: "The older we get, the greater becomes our inclination to give thanks, especially heavenwards. We feel more strongly than we could possibly have ever felt before that life is a free gift...and every hour...an unexpected gift to be gratefully received."

Pierre Teilhard de Chardin: "I thank you my God for having in a thousand ways led my eyes to discover the immense simplicity of things. Little by little, through the irresistable development of those yearnings you implanted in me as a child, and through the awakenings of spirit I owe the successive initiations gentle and terrible, which you caused me to undergo; through all these I have been brought to the point where I can no longer see anything, nor any longer breathe outside that milieu in which all is made one."

It seems clear to me that the Holy Spirit is calling all of us, more and more, to a life of forgiveness and thanksgiving. The prayer of thanksgiving is itself the prelude to the prayer of praise. Then when we pause in quiet praise of God, the need for words diminishes and we enter an atmosphere of joyful silence. This quiet time is restful and full of peace. It is called the gift of contemplation, and it flourishes in a grateful heart.

* * *

No heaven can come to us unless our hearts find rest in today. Take heaven.

No peace lies in the future which is not hidden in this precious little instant. Take peace.

The gloom of the world is but a shadow. Behind it, yet within our reach is joy. Take joy.

There is a radiance and courage in darkness could we but see; and to see, we have only to look.

Life is so generous a giver, but we, judging its gifts by their coverings, cast them away as ugly or heavy or hard.

Remove the covering and you will find beneath it a living splendor woven of love and wisdom and power.
Welcome it, greet it, and you touch the angel's hand that brings it.

Everything we call a trial, a sorrow, a duty, believe me,
that angel's hand is there, and the wonder of an
overshadowing Presence. . .
Life is so full of meaning and purpose, so full of beauty
beneath its covering that you will find earth but cloaks
for your heaven.
Courage then, to claim it, that is all!

Fra Angelico (15th century monk)

CHAPTER FIVE

Pray

This, then, is what I pray, kneeling before the Father...
Out of His infinite glory
may He give you the power through His Spirit
for your hidden self to grow strong
so that Christ may live in your hearts
through faith.

And then, planted in love and built on love,
you will with all the saints have strength
to grasp the breadth and the length,
the height and the depth;
until, knowing the love of Christ,
which is beyond all knowledge,
you are filled with the utter fullness of God.

(Eph. 3:14–19)

For most people prayer is asking God for things they need. But the scriptures assure us that He knows all our needs.

May I make a suggestion? When you talk to God, think big! Ask Him for the grace of holiness, even if you don't fully understand it. Think about being a saint, a great saint. It's never too late. Some of the greatest saints were once rogues but they changed radically. Through God's grace they became holy:

> *Because they were cheerful*
> *   when it was difficult to be cheerful;*
> *Patient when it was difficult to be patient;*
> *Because they pushed forward*
> *   when they wanted to stand still;*
> *They kept silent when they wanted to talk;*
> *They were agreeable*
> *   when they wanted to be disagreeable.*
> *That was all. It was quite simple and always will be.*

What strikes me in all this is the importance of the passive virtues: restraint, patience, silence. St. Paul's famous commentary on love repeats the same theme:

> *Charity is patient, is kind, charity does not envy, is not pretentious, is not puffed up, is not ambitious, is not self-seeking, is not provoked, thinks no evil, does not rejoice over wickedness but rejoices with the truth; bears with all things, believes all things, hopes all things, endures all things.*
>
> (1 Cor. 13:4–7)

How much of your life is filled with waiting, enduring, holding back? Most of us do a lot of waiting as a matter of routine. It doesn't seem to be especially meritorious or sanctifying, but apparently in God's view it is. I think of so many good people who suffer the humiliation of being taken for granted, being used, even unintentionally, by the people they love. They endure these things because they're holy. The very enduring of it is a beautiful prayer to God.

John Milton, in his sonnet on blindness, wrote these famous words: "They also serve who only stand and wait." The service of love is so often a kind of waiting, a kind of praying in "unspeakable groans."

God waits. The world He made is filled with waiting. Waiting is one of the primary laws of nature. Winter waits for spring. Buds wait for warmth. The earth waits for rain. Nothing in life comes to instant maturity. The value of waiting is far superior to a mindless activism. All things begin as a tiny seed, waiting to grow to full stature. Joy is often one of the fruits of waiting. Dante described hope as "a waiting with certitude." There is ultimate meaning to all our waiting. One day we will be united with God in heaven.

Pray now for the grace to wait openly before the Holy Spirit. Sometimes it is in the silence of waiting that we learn to reach the depths of our own being. Sometimes doing nothing can be the greatest service. Sometimes just being where you're supposed to be when you want to run away, might be the holiest prayer you've ever prayed.

Each person is unique, so each person has his or her own distinctive way of praying.

Prayer is as individual as a handprint. Kindergarten youngsters in one Milwaukee class made individual hand-prints as gifts for Father's Day. One little girl presented hers to her dad and said, "This is me. There's no other hand like mine in the world."

She was so right. No two people are alike; no two peo-ple approach the Lord in exactly the same way. No one else can give to God what you can give. You don't have to imitate anyone else to please God, you just have to be yourself, and make a reasonable effort to be good.

For most of us, learning to pray is a lifetime struggle. As we open ourselves to God and as our understanding of Him deepens, our approach to Him may change. This is a normal function of growth. Sometimes God feels very distant; at other times He is very close. Forget about your feelings for a moment. Try to be objective.

Think of a cloudy day. You may not feel the sun's warmth on a cloudy day, but you know it's there. God's love is like that. God's love is unchanging. His love is present whether you feel it or not. You may feel He has abandoned you but His love is as constant as the sun.

> *Your love is better than life itself.*
>
> (Ps. 63:3)

Talking to God is like talking with a friend. A friend is one who accepts us as we are, when we're at our best or at our worst. God is like that. He sees through the unreal image we sometimes present to others, even to ourselves. He accepts us "as is."

He understands your weaknesses, your hidden thoughts, everything. So just be yourself and talk to Him.

You say you have too many distractions? I know, I do too. Our minds are going all the time, thinking about all kinds of things: frivolous, serious, loving, mean, painful, joyful. Some we would share with no one. Writer Henri Nouwen suggests that we turn these thoughts into prayer:

> We convert our unceasing thinking into unceasing prayer when we move from a self-centered monologue into a God-centered dialogue. This requires that we turn all our thoughts into a conversation. The main question therefore, is not so much what we think, but to whom we present our thoughts.

Prayer is giving all our thoughts to God, opening to Him the secret places, the corners we guard.

You know me through and through, from having watched my bones take shape when I was being formed in secret.

(Ps. 139:15)

Talking to God helps you to feel His strength in your weakness. Don't be ashamed of the things you've done and keep on doing. Weakness can bring you closer to God. Once you admit you're a sinner, you can ask Him to help you with His strength. St. Paul taught all of us to do exactly that:

I was given a thorn in the flesh, an angel of Satan to beat me and stop me from getting too proud. About this thing, I have pleaded with the Lord three times for it to leave me, but He has said, "My grace is enough for you. My power is at its best in weakness."

(2 Cor. 12:7-9)

The Lord is waiting for your trust. You can give Him your weakness, your problems, your weariness. He is ready to make His power available. You have only to ask. But once you do, be quiet and learn to listen.

To listen means to be alert, open, quiet. God speaks to us in many ways: in the beauty of His world, in the pain of life, in the comfort of others, or in their call for help. Listen to God in the world about you:

What you do for the least of My brothers and sisters you do for Me.

(Mt. 25:40)

Listen for Him to tell you where you fit into His plan of things.

Listen for clues as to how you can make the world around you a better place.

Listen so that you'll know what it means to be a bearer of divine love.

Is it possible to enjoy God? It surely is. In fact, when you really know the good news—that God is Unchanging Love—you can't help but rejoice in His presence.

* * *

Every day an old man came to the church to pray. He always sat quietly in the last pew. One day the parish priest decided to ask him about it. "What do you say to God in all that time you spend in church?"

The man smiled and answered, "I don't say anything. He just looks at me and I look at Him. We enjoy one another."

Enjoying the Lord in silence; that's contemplation. It is a relaxing love relationship. The mind rests and the heart is full of joy.

Contemplation begins where other prayer leaves off. In contemplation there are no words, no actions, no thoughts. Our heart is open before God. We receive His love and enjoy His presence.

One idea that might help you to contemplate more comfortably is to believe in God's union with you and your union with Him. Remember He created you, making you His own. This union has always depended more on His love for you than on your love for Him. It is He who desired you first; it is He who calls you to Himself. Once you truly believe He is within you, open yourself to Him, relax, rest in His love.

Enjoying the Lord is as close to heaven as we can get here on earth. Cardinal Desire Mercier of Belgium (1851–1926) wrote a lovely prayer which I have quoted often. It has helped many people, I hope it will do the same for you.

"I will reveal to you the secret of sanctity and of happiness. If for five minutes a day you are able to quiet your imagination, to close your eyes to the things of the senses, to enter within your soul which is the temple of the Holy Spirit, and there to speak with this Divine Spirit:

> *O Holy Spirit, soul of my soul...*
> *Guide me, strengthen me, console me,*
>   *tell me what to do...*
> *I promise to submit*
>   *to whatever you desire of me*
> *and to accept everything you allow to happen to*
>   *me.*
>   *Let me only know Your will...*

"If you do this your life will flow happily, serene and consoled even in the midst of pain."

* * *

Prayer is not the exclusive property of Christians. It is in the nature of man to pray. Rabbi Abraham Joshua Heschel put it this way:

Prayer is not a stratagem for occasional use, a refuge to resort to now and then. It is rather like an established residence for the innermost self. All things have a home; the bird has a nest, the fox has a hole, the bee has a hive. *A soul without prayer is a soul without a home...* To pray is to open a door where both God and the soul may enter.

Let me illustrate the role of joy in our prayer life with this story about two Buddhist monks.

The two monks belonged to different Buddhist traditions and lived miles apart. The first monk was somber. He prayed all day long in deep, motionless silence. The second monk was playful. He sang his praises to the Lord as he danced around a huge sycamore tree in the monastery garden.

One day an angel appeared to the first monk and said, "I have come from God and you have permission to ask Him one question. What will your question be?" The somber monk paused thoughtfully and then asked: "How many more lives must I live before I will attain self-realization?"

The angel left him and appeared to the monk who was singing and dancing before the Lord. The angel said, "I have come from God and you have permission to ask Him one question. What is your question?" Without hesitation, the joyful monk responded, "How many more lives must I live before I will attain self-realization?" And with that the angel disappeared.

One week later the angel returned to the first monk with the answer. "You must live three more lives before you will attain self-realization." The somber monk broke down in tears of desolation, "Three more lives, three more lives," he wept. "Oh no, no. Three more lives."

The angel left him and soon after appeared to the dancing monk. "I have your answer," he said. "Do you see that tree around which you have been dancing and singing your praises to God?"

"Yes," said the joyful monk.

"You must live as many more lives as there are leaves on that tree, and only then will you attain self-realization," said the angel.

The monk looked up at the tree and shouted happily, "Why, there must be 10,000 leaves on that tree. Only 10,000 more lives and I will attain self-realization." And he sang and danced with even more exuberance.

Suddenly the voice of God thundered from heaven. "My son, this day you have attained self-realization!"

This parable deserves a good bit of meditation. If you see what I see you'll agree that Christians believe the same simple truth as Buddhists, and many others of God's children: "In His will is our peace and joy." The moment of total acceptance becomes the moment of total liberation.

A Creed for Those Who Have Suffered

I asked God for strength,
   that I might achieve
I was made weak,
   that I might learn humbly to obey...

I asked for health,
   that I might do greater things
I was given infirmity,
   that I might do better things...

I asked for riches,
   that I might be happy
I was given poverty,
   that I might be wise...

I asked for power,
   that I might have the praise of men
I was given weakness,
   that I might feel the need of God...

I asked for all things,
   that I might enjoy life
I was given life,
   that I might enjoy all things...

I got nothing that I asked for—
   but everything I had hoped for
Almost despite myself,
   my unspoken prayers were answered
I am among all men, most richly blessed!

An Unknown Confederate Soldier

CHAPTER SIX

Go

As a young man I felt a strong attraction for the priest-hood, but I held back. I was afraid to assume the many burdens; afraid of all the alligators in the swamp of life; afraid of failing. I couldn't see the outcome of such a choice. It took me about seven years of inner turmoil, from high school through college and military service, before I had the courage to trust Him enough, the courage to say "yes" to God's call. I never regretted my decision. Once I decided to put my hand in His, I knew I would be safe, I knew I had something more dependable than human assurances. He would be responsible for my life from now on in a special way.

Fear and hesitation can still clutter my consciousness from time to time, but on a deeper level I am aware of His strength, and I am not afraid.

It's difficult to explain how you can be confident about the essential things while still experiencing some nervous ness and anxiety on the surface. Going forth in love from situation to situation can still be a frightening challenge, but when I am armed with prayer, things seem to work out. More things are wrought by prayer than anyone can imagine.

So when the Lord asked me to go, I went. It took me years to get started but I finally got going. But where was I to go? It was simple: go to those in need—the poor, the hungry, the lonely, with all the risks such going implied.

I learned that His love in me impels me to show mercy when I want to be resentful. It's His love that induces me to sacrifice my time, my comfort, when others reach out and I want to be alone. No big deal, it's just part of life. However imperfectly I perform, I know it is the Lord working in me.

Sometimes it gets thick. Love can be "a harsh and dreadful thing," says Dostoevski. We know from life's experiences that wherever there is love there is the cross. No need to go into detail, we all experience the pain of trying to love well.

* * *

To understand God's love again we look to Jesus. His life has affected countless individuals down through the ages and each one of us has responded to Him in our own way. We asked some people the question, "For you, who is Jesus Christ?" Here are just a few of the replies, all taken from the Christopher book, *And You, Who Do You Say I Am?*

Jesus Christ is not only my closest and most intimate friend, but He is manifested almost daily, forcefully (and beautifully) in the people with whom I come in contact. "Ordinary" days are made extraordinary by chance encounters, by human intercourse that moves the heart or lifts the spirit or is shaped like laughter.

Maureen Cannon, poet

He came to enlighten my early years with the radiation of His power, like a dawning sun; He whispered to me the kind of words that make a destiny: "Come, and follow Me! Little by little I discovered and verified anew the lightning truth of Jesus' words, "Whoever sees Me sees the Father!"

Cardinal Leon Joseph Suenens
Retired Primate of Belgium

I am a musician: for me the meaning of Jesus in my life is tied to all the struggles and hard work the life of an artist demands. Through my music, I try to communicate to others what is in my heart: the Lord's grace, His gifts and love.

Karen Olsen, music student

We're all unique and we respond to Jesus differently. He revealed much about Himself not only in what He said, but what He did. We can understand better by studying the people He sought out: the lepers, the Samaritans, the prostitutes, the publicans. When you see how Jesus pursued the outcast, the secret of His joy will begin to unfold.

Jesus rejected the prevalent idea that all people with physical disabilities or a disease such as leprosy were afflicted that way as a direct punishment for sin. That's what people believed in those times. A disabled person was considered defiled, contemptible to God. Jesus reacted strongly against this cruel prejudice.

As He went along, He saw a man who had been blind from birth. His disciples asked, "Rabbi, who sinned, this man or his parents, for him to have been born blind?" Jesus thundered: "Neither he nor his parents sinned."

(Jn. 9:1–3)

His whole ministry was a reaching out to the underdog. In so doing He swept aside the taboos of His times. Consider the Samaritans. Jesus violated the law just by talking with them—they were people of mixed blood who were rejected for marrying outside their family heritage. But Jesus accepted them as children of God.

Consider the prostitutes. The prostitute is a symbol of all morally broken people. Jesus rebuked those who condemned them. He always loved the sinner, but condemned the sin. "Go and sin no more...," but as He said those words He gently reached out in love.

Remember when Jesus came to the home of Simon the Pharisee; a woman "who had a bad name in town" came and kissed His feet, wiping her tears from His feet with her hair. His hosts were scandalized, but Jesus ignored them as He accepted her lovingly:

For this reason I tell you that her sins, her many sins are forgiven because she has loved much. He who forgives little shows little love.

(Lk. 7:47–48)

There's that word "forgiveness" again. Do you see the pattern? The Lord teaches by example.

Jesus loves losers. Even in choosing His apostles He picked losers. Levi, later called Matthew, was a Publican, one of many mercenaries who collected taxes for the despised Romans. These people were considered traitors by the Pharisees; they were men of greed who, according to the scribes and priests, lacked faith.

Jesus didn't disagree with that harsh judgment. He admitted there were sinners among them, but He made the point that a man of God does not condemn, but seeks out the lost sheep.

...A number of tax-collectors and sinners came to sit

at the table with Jesus and His disciples. When the Phari-
sees saw this, they said to His disciples, "Why does your
Master eat with tax-collectors and sinners?" Jesus heard
this and replied, "It is not the healthy who need the doc-
tor, but the sick. Go and learn the meaning of the words,
'What I want is mercy, not sacrifice.' And indeed I did not
come to call the virtuous, but sinners."

(Mt. 9:10–13)

Where are we to go? We are to "go about doing good"
as Jesus did. Did Jesus spend His energies building buildings, paying off debts, feathering the nests of the apostles?
No. Jesus went to help those in need; sinners, the under-
privileged, the outcast. He went to those on the fringes of
society to give solace and comfort, and He had the credentials to get our attention:

The blind see again, and the lame walk, lepers are
cleansed, the deaf hear, the dead are raised to life, and the
Good News is proclaimed to the poor . . .

(Mt. 11:5–6)

* * *

When we speak of "going forth" we look to Jesus and
begin to understand what it means. The church is Jesus
extended in time, and this is the church's mission. The
words "Help carry one another's burdens, in this way you
will fulfill the law of Jesus Christ" (Gal. 6:6), begin to
have deeper meaning.

In helping others Jesus had to overturn respected traditions. He paid a great price for His love of neighbor. In so
doing, He revealed the Father as a merciful God, a God
who would risk all to save His beloved. Jesus challenged
anyone who presumed to limit God's love. He insisted

that God loves unconditionally and universally. The elders of His time were completely baffled. For them, fidelity to the law was the prime requirement and the only security for obtaining God's blessing. They really didn't understand. But Jesus did. He explained it to a Pharisee named Nicodemus, who visited Jesus secretly because he was afraid of being seen in His company.

"Rabbi, we know You are from God, for no one could perform the signs that You do unless God were with Him," said Nicodemus. (Jn. 3:1-2) They spoke briefly, then Jesus said, "...God has sent His son into the world not to condemn the world, but so that through Him the world might be saved." (Jn. 3:17)

Jesus spoke with such knowledge and power about "God the Father," He awakened a deep curiosity in His apostles. Philip once asked, "Lord, let us see the Father and then we shall be satisfied." In one of the most important texts in the bible, Jesus replies, "Have I been with you all this time, Philip, and you still do not know Me? To have seen Me is to have seen the Father... The words I say to you, I do not speak from Myself. It is the Father, living in Me, who is doing this work." (Jn. 14:8-10)

Jesus does what the Father wants. He goes where the Father asks Him to go. The words and actions of Jesus therefore are privileged channels of communication for us. God the Father speaks through His words and actions. In Jesus we have the means of penetrating the mystery of God.

Not everyone can go forth exactly as Jesus did. Some are too weak, too limited; some are too sick or too emotionally drained. Some are in too much pain. But Jesus knows our pain. He shed light on the mystery of suffering for us.

The Lord did not come to suppress suffering or deny it, but rather to fill it with His presence. He taught us that love and suffering may go hand in hand, but they lead to joy. Jesus knew His actions would invite the derision of powerful enemies. But when His Father asked Him to go and teach it meant He would have to sacrifice Himself in the process. His reply was an agony of human resistance, but the end result was perfect obedience. "Not My will but Thine be done."

Why did He do it? Why did He give Himself over to such a fate?

He died for all so that those who live should no longer live for themselves but for Him, who died and was raised to life for their sake.

(2 Cor. 5:15)

He died to lead us away from selfishness; He died that we might live for others as He did. In His sacrifice we begin to penetrate the mystery of spiritual joy. Jesus on the very night before His passion and death said, *I tell you these things that your joy may be full.* (Jn. 15:15)

He showed us that the way to joy is through spiritual self-surrender.

* * *

In times past, many Christians were merely sociological Christians—people who were Christians because their society was.

Today that climate of faith is disappearing. Now each one has to accept Jesus or reject Him on the basis of a personal decision, and His words are therefore even more important. We all know that to follow Him sincerely is not easy.

In the Sermon on the Mount, Jesus delivers the heart of His message, the eight Beatitudes. Again we turn to those mysterious words. They are all different aspects of one truth, all mysterious keys to that elusive mystery of spiritual happiness which is the fruit of selfless surrender to God's will. Jesus encourages us to "go" as He did, to save that which is lost.

"How happy are the poor in spirit: theirs is the kingdom of heaven." He implied in this teaching that the meek, the comforters, the merciful, and the peacemakers—these are the favored ones of God. He teaches us that caring for a neighbor is not only tending to his wounds after the beating has taken place, but also means taking pains to see that he won't be beaten again. It may mean standing up sternly to his oppressor.

Happy are those who hunger and thirst for what is right, they shall be satisfied. Happy are those who are persecuted in the cause of right; theirs is the kingdom of heaven.

(Mt. 5:3–10)

Believing in the Beatitudes is not fashionable, because it leads to trouble. Ridicule can be stinging; being called a bleeding heart, a do-gooder, a coward is not enjoyable. Everyone working for human rights has been maligned at one time or another. They are called fools. But is imitating the Lord foolishness? Was Jesus a fool for obeying the Father?

Even so, there is a need for balance in activism. Not all aspects of activism are worthy of praise; excesses often mar high-sounding goals. In his encyclical *Rich in Mercy*, Pope John Paul II alluded to this problem: "It is obvious in fact that in the name of an alleged justice (for example, historical or class justice) the neighbor is sometimes destroyed, killed, deprived of liberty, or stripped of fundamental human rights." The history of atheistic Marxism is filled with such abuses. Marxists are great protestors, but they are also great killers when they take power. They have high-sounding rhetoric but they hold human life cheaply.

Good people are led astray, but we can't be discouraged. There is always grace, and Jesus promised to send the Holy Spirit to help us discern His will.

The Holy Spirit issues an invitation to each of us. It is as though He says, "you are unique and unrepeatable." When God touches you, you will blossom in a way different from anyone else.

A teaching of St. Cyril of Jerusalem (386 A.D.) sheds some light on the way the Holy Spirit enables us to find our spiritual fulfillment. He compared the spirit of God to water. It was an image he chose because of Christ's words, "The water that I shall give him will become in him a spring of water welling up to eternal life." (Jn. 4:14)

"Water," said St. Cyril, "comes down from heaven as rain, and although it is always the same in itself, it produces many different effects; one in the palm tree, another in the vine, and so on, throughout the whole of creation. It does not come down now as one thing, now as another, but while remaining essentially the same, it adapts itself to the nature and need of every creature that receives it. In the same way the Holy Spirit, whose nature is always the same, simple and indivisible, apportions grace to each man as He wills."

Cyril's idea is that our basic natural gifts are enhanced by the Holy Spirit:

The Spirit makes one person a teacher of divine truth, inspires another to prophesy... The Spirit strengthens one person's self-control, shows another how to help the poor, teaches another to fast and lead a life of asceticism, makes another oblivious to the needs of the body, trains another for martyrdom... In each person the Spirit reveals His presence in a particular way for the common good.

From this we see that it is possible to be weak in one or more areas, while still being gifted in another. No one receives all the gifts, but each of us receives some gifts.

Strange isn't it, how some people feel diminished when they come across real holiness or outstanding generosity in another? But that's being unfair to oneself. We can't all be like John the Baptist, fasting in the desert; or Joan of Arc, leading an army in battle. Every saint is unique, every person different.

As I reflect on the teaching of St. Cyril, I realize how important it is for us to thank God for what we have, whatever it is. The variety of gifts we all possess in common gives balance to the Church. And since the gifts of the Spirit are given for the common good, we can rejoice heartily in any of the gifts God gives to others. So count your blessings.

. . . We have received the Spirit that comes from God, to teach us to understand the gifts that He has given us.
(1 Cor. 2:12)

Jesus tells us "go forth" in very specific terms.
Be poor in spirit
Be meek and humble
Be a comfort to others
Be a seeker after justice
Be merciful
Be clean of heart
Be a peacemaker
Be willing to suffer for justice's sake.

It is in this spirit that we at The Christophers believe:

■ Governments are not too powerful to be reformed.

■ Institutions are not too big to be changed.

■ Positive, constructive action can overcome evil.

We firmly believe that, with the help of God, all things are possible.

The Christopher Message

Convinced that spiritually motivated individuals can bring constructive change to the world, Father James Keller, a Maryknoll priest, founded The Christophers in 1945. I am honored to be his successor in this work. The Christophers try to cut across denominational lines and appeal to people of all faiths, motivating them to accept personal responsibility to make this a more just and moral society, to make the world a happier place for all God's children.

Thomas Carlyle, the historian, was right when he said: ". . . Empires fall or civilizations decline, not necessarily through some colossal criminality, but from multitudinous cases of petty betrayal or individual neglect."

We try to teach people the skills that enable them to "speak the truth with love." Our News Notes and leadership courses cover a wide variety of topics: how to communicate, how to write effectively, how to make your point at a meeting, how to take specific action to change your world for the better. These are all ways to obey the supreme law, ways to love God and serve your neighbor.

The Christophers emphasize these points:

■ You have a job to do that nobody else can do.

■ You can help raise public standards in school, at work, in your community.

■ You can promote the rights of all.

Nearly all great human achievements begin with the inspiration and hard work of one dedicated person. When individuals are responsible, society prospers; when they lose their sense of responsiblity, society decays.

Much of the present chaos results from the tendency of the average good person to "let George do it." Those who fall into the trap of believing that institutions are too big to change forget the lessons of history. What The Christophers are trying to say is summed up in a prayer written by the great Cardinal John Henry Newman of England. I would like to share that prayer with you:

God has created me to do Him some definite service; He has committed some work to me which He has not committed to another. . .
Therefore I will trust Him.
Whatever, wherever I am, I can never be thrown away. If I am in sickness, my sickness may serve Him; in perplexity, my perplexity may serve Him; if I am in sorrow, my sorrow may serve Him. . .

Father Keller encouraged everyone to become a carrier of Divine Love—a Christbearer:

Needed:
More to improve, fewer merely to disapprove.
More doers, fewer talkers.
More to say "it can be done."
More to inspire others with confidence,
    fewer to throw cold water on anyone taking

even one step in the right direction.
More to get into the thick of things
   and do something,
   fewer to sit on the sidelines
   merely to find fault.
More to point out what's right with the world,
   fewer to keep harping
   on what's wrong with the world.
More to be interested in "lighting candles,"
   fewer in blowing them out.

CHAPTER SEVEN

Teach

Jesus taught us to go out of ourselves and unite with others in bonds of caring. Don't let your possessions hold you back, He said. Leave everything behind and "follow Me." The gospel injunction of renunciation is at the heart of all Christian teaching. Jesus told us to lose our life in order to gain it.

To lose one's life for God is to apply oneself to the task of growing as a human being. We share as Christians in the task of building the kingdom of justice, peace and love. Joy, then, is one of the by-products of that effort, one of the fruits of a good life. Just as the tiny seed must enter the ground in order to bear fruit in the future, so too are we called by the Holy Spirit to a life of giving, a life of sharing.

Experience teaches that the Spirit often leads us to the place we would least fancy for ourselves. When the cross appears, our life changes. Either we recoil or we plunge ahead. By faith we know that the cross is good. But our nature always recoils from suffering. Those who preach the gospel of Jesus undoubtedly meet resistance, or worse, rejection. People don't like to lose control of their environment.

I know one woman who claimed she lost her faith because God was silent during a particularly painful time of her life. He never answered her prayers, she said. But she was wrong. God is not silent. God is never silent for those who know how to listen; those who know where to look. Let me explain.

Faith is knowledge. One either knows or does not know that the supreme revelation of God is Jesus Christ. To know Jesus is to begin to understand God. Whether or not you get daily briefings from on high, however comforting they might be, is not the issue. To know Jesus is to know where to look to find the meaning of human happiness.

The Christian vision of reality goes against our natural inclinations. We are all too human, and we easily lose sight of God's point of view. No wonder some people claim to have lost their faith. But perhaps they never had real faith in the first place. Perhaps they never understood that suffering can and often does coexist with divine favor. Jesus taught us that on the cross.

When a person gets angry with God, God's nature doesn't change. He is Unchanging Love. He always returns good for evil, love for hatred. We, on the other hand, establish our own criteria for God. If He does not do as we expect, we walk away from Him. Ultimately it is we who create our own hell as we withdraw from God's love. The flower needs the sun.

But God is patient. He looks with compassion on all human aberrations and returns pure love.

It's easy to teach book knowledge but teaching Christianity is difficult. Why? Because the Christian life is not so much a philosophy or a body of doctrine to be taught, as it is a life to be lived, a life centered on Jesus. A joyful life can be pursued in many ways, but the Christian has a special advantage in knowing where to look. We look to Jesus. Our faith in Him gives us a knowledge and an understanding of ourselves and the world around us, a knowledge illuminated by His light.

Teaching the Christian view of reality is best done by living it. We instruct others best by our actions, and then our words have the ring of truth. Teaching is not so much communicating a list of definitions. Teaching has the more pragmatic goal of helping others to live life as God created us to live it.

How to live the Christian life? That is the question.

How to love and receive love in communion with others? How to forgive those who offend us? How to pray to the Father with Jesus in the Holy Spirit? How to go out to those in need, without looking for praise or thanks?

Love, forgive, pray, go, teach—these are the words of life. Jesus calls us to do all this in the light of faith. He gives us a new view of reality, and we try to respond in a spirit of love. God's love is the Good News of the gospel. But there are anti-gospel forces in the world. The evil one sows seeds of unrest, seeds of hatred. The Christ-bearer is aware of the enemy at all times.

There is a longstanding trend in education today which teaches children that there is no right, there is no wrong, but only what's right for you; that there is no God—that man is his own God.

This trend affects more than education; it is a widespread phenomenon permeating all of modern life. It even influences personal relationships.

The philosophical basis for the trend is called secular humanism.

The secular humanist places man at the center of the

universe, designating him as the supreme ruler of human destiny. However, the Christian teacher places Christ at the center of the cosmos and recognizes Him as the Way, the Truth and the Life.

The secular humanist says, "Religious training should be abolished," even while fostering a creed of his own. Not only is the Humanist Creed a set of beliefs in the truest sense, but secular humanism has been accorded the status of religious belief by the courts and by society.

The Oxford English Dictionary's shortest definition of secular humanism is "the religion of humanity." Webster defines it as: "a doctrine, set of attitudes, or way of life centered on human interests or values; a philosophy that rejects supernaturalism, regards man as a natural object and asserts the essential dignity and worth of a man and his capacity to achieve self-realization through the use of reason and the scientific method;—a religion subscribing to these beliefs."

The appeal of secular humanism is in the idea that man shapes his own destiny for better or worse and that he does it all alone.

The notion of Divine Providence, of being in God's hands, is unacceptable to the atheistic humanist.

* * *

The Humanist Creed was first codified in 1933 when American humanists, under the leadership of John Dewey, philosopher and educator, drew up the "Humanist Manifesto." The Manifesto was loaded with hostility against traditional religion. It held that there is no God; that religious belief is an enemy of human progress, and that only rationality and science can save us.

Forty years later, in 1973, the Manifesto was updated but it preserved the same negative spirit. Most of its major

themes were again repeated in the latest humanist declara-
tion published in 1980. Here are a few of those themes:

> We find insufficient evidence for belief in the existence
> of a supernatural, it is either meaningless or irrelevant
> to the question of the survival and fulfillment of the
> human race.

> Traditional, dogmatic or authoritarian religions...
> do a disservice to the human species.

Obviously the enemy has planted some bad seed and
it's flourishing today. But where did this anti-gospel
begin? Evil has been around from the beginning, but
more recently it has been the outgrowth of the intellectual
revolution shaped by 19th century philosophers and
social scientists. Here, briefly, are some key dates and the
men in the forefront of that revolution.

■ (1830) Ludwig Feuerbach, sometimes called the
father of the anti-God movement, popularized ideas
such as these: "The turning point in history will be the
moment when man becomes aware that the only God of
man is man himself." "We have to replace the love of
God with the love of man."

■ (1848) Karl Marx wrote The Communist Manifesto
partly on the basis of a draft prepared by his friend,
Frederick Engels. "Religion is the opium of the people."
Both Marx and Engels were in their late 20s at the time
and they were influenced by Feuerbach. Engels wrote:
"At one blow the god-myth was demolished. We all
straightaway became Feuerbachians."

■ (1851) Auguste Comte: "The great revolution of the
West...proclaims and at the same time ensures 'the

hopeless effeteness' of the reign of God...God is unquestionably gone forever."

■ (1855) Emile Soisset: "Herr Feuerbach offers Christian Europe a new God to worship...the human race."

■ (1888) Friedrich Nietzche: "God is dead. It is we who have killed him...We are the assassins of God...We are at war against the Christian ideal, against the doctrine which makes beatitudes and salvation the aim of life."

Nietzche expressed the inevitable connection between ideas and actions; "Thoughts come before actions," he said, "as lightning before thunder." First come the thinkers, then the executioners.

Hitler idolized Nietzche and became his iron fist. In the Soviet Union gods were made of Marx and Lenin; soon after, Stalin began his murderous climb to power. He built the world's first atheistic state on wholesale murder.

Two world wars, massacres, slave labor camps and holocausts—these are the legacies of militant atheism. There is more than intellectual error and deception in all this. There is the presence of the evil one. In the book of Genesis we see that God reveals His word; but the serpent speaks the anti-word. The same drama is being played today. Good is called evil, and evil good. Writing in *The Drama of Atheistic Humanism*, Father Henri De Lubac said:

Atheistic humanism was bound to end in bankruptcy —if man takes himself as a God, he can for a time cherish the illusion that he freed himself, but it is a fleeting exultation. In reality, he has merely abased God, and it is not long before he abases himself.

The French philosopher Maritain, commenting on the cause of modern atheism, had this to say:

> At the root of it, and chiefly through the fault of a Christian world unfaithful to its principles, there is a deep resentment (and that is the tragedy of it) against Christianity itself...Resentment against those who have not been able to give effect to the truth of which they were the bearers; resentment which is rebounding against the truth itself.

Secular humanism is a false teaching. In its attempts to liberate human beings, it has failed to provide the basis for the ordinary social virtues which involve discipline and self-control. There is no God, no after life, no need to pursue anything but the good life. But we have to believe that the secular humanist trend can be turned around.

At the age of 34, for instance, William Murray, son of Madalyn Murray O'Hair, apologized publicly for his role in the court battle that led to the U.S. Supreme Court ruling banning state-mandated prayer in public schools. Murray realized something was missing in his life. He became a Christian, saying: "Atheism is an ego-centered, materialistic-minded dogma."

The Lord was made flesh—He became our brother—to save us from our pride, our disorder, our selfish secular selves. He tells us that indeed we have great value, eternal value, that each one of us is precious. He tells us of God's Unchanging Love. He too speaks of justice, human dignity, freedom.

Taking this world seriously, making it a happier, better place to live for all people, was His concern. Jesus shows us what it is to be truly human:

Blessed are the poor in spirit, for theirs is the kingdom

*of heaven...Blessed are the meek, for they shall inherit
the earth...Blessed are the pure in heart, for they shall
see God...Blessed are the peacemakers, for they shall be
called sons of God.*

(Mt. 5:3–10)

The Beatitudes, considered folly by Nietzche and his
followers, are the blueprint of a true Christian humanism
where people learn to care for one another.

The Golden Rule is not exclusively Christian, however.
We have much in common with other traditions. Under-
girding our society, for instance, are some basic Judaic-
Christian principles:

■ Belief in the existence of a personal God who has
spoken to the world.

■ Acceptance of the Ten Commandments and the
Golden Rule as revealed rules of conduct for all.

■ Respect for the sacred character of every individual
and his/her right to life and liberty.

■ Acknowledgment of the sanctity of marriage and the
family.

■ Derivation of the human rights of every person from
God, not from the state.

To maintain these values all believers have to work together. It is true that "sin has increased but grace has far
surpassed it." (Rom. 5:20)

As we turn to Jesus for strength, let's remember that religion should foster love and respect across sectarian
lines. Whenever hatred enters, it is not from God.

Let's avoid the "wagon-train" mentality where small groups close in on themselves to fight against the outside world. They often become their own worst enemies.

Pray for atheists, agnostics and secular humanists. They are human beings whom God loves and wants to save. He is the same God who became man and sought after the lost sheep of Israel. But in loving those poisoned by the enemy, don't be confused by their benign-sounding philosophy. The anti-God movement is full of half-truths which can deceive more effectively than outright lies.

Stand fast in your faith. Speak up, write that letter, resist evil—at work, at meetings, in school, wherever the anti-God movement is promoted. Protect your children against secular humanist ideas. Strengthen the bonds of love in your home. Pray for God's help in all circumstances. Care about one another. Listen to one another. Give time and attention to one another as needs arise.

The teacher lives and works in the here and now, but always with the vision of hope for a future victory:

Eye has not seen, ear has not heard, nor has it so much as dawned on man what God has prepared for those who love Him.

(1 Cor. 2:10)

And so it becomes clearer: teaching truth is not the exclusive domain of preachers and teachers. We teach, for better or worse, wherever we are, even without intending to. Again I return to Cardinal Newman's prayer:

I have my mission...
  I am a link in a chain, a bond of connection
  between persons.
He has not created me for naught,
  I shall do good, I shall do His work.

I shall be an angel of peace,
*   a preacher of truth in my own place*
*   while not intending it—*
if I do but keep His commandments.

Teaching Christianity is best done by those who live the Christian life themselves. Lovers are the best teachers.

I shall pass through this life but once.
Any good, therefore, that I can do,
*   Or any kindness I can show to any fellow creature,*
*   Let me do it now*
*   Let me not defer or neglect it,*
For I shall not pass this way again.

Etienne de Grellet

PART II

*The joy of the Lord
is your strength*
Nehemiah 8:10

CHAPTER EIGHT

Accepting the Challenge

Jesus gave us a balanced spiritual program. He did not encourage a self-absorbed, self-cultivating brand of spirituality. Nor did He advocate religion as a vehicle exclusively designed to promote social action.

When one aspect of the truth is exaggerated it can easily grow into a lie. Both prayer and action need to be balanced. These values are not the creation of man. However great man's works may be in concept or execution, his work is merely human. Balance is part of Divine Wisdom.

The social betterment of mankind is certainly a goal of Christian living. Bringing about more order, beauty, happiness in life is a Christian duty; and insofar as these are the fruits of love, they should flourish wherever the Body of Christ is found.

But the service of one's neighbor, however noble it may be, can never substitute for the central spiritual challenge of our lives, the supreme law's first concern: to love God with your whole heart, mind and soul.

We are called to change the world, yes. One person can make a difference, yes, and sometimes a decisive difference, but our power to effect the very change we seek is dependent on the One who calls us to service.

In our literature we at The Christophers always stress the phrase: "With God's help." We pray. The soul needs silence and solitude to draw from God's immense power. Without prayer there will be no spiritual perception, no spiritual power.

Love, forgive, pray, go, teach: all five words taken together help us to understand the fullness of the gospel.

Jesus committed to His followers the main task of preaching the gospel. How? In three ways—by our prayers, our words, and our actions. In prayer we receive power; in our words and actions, we give it away. It's like breathing in and breathing out.

Evelyn Underhill observed that "The soul's two activities of reception and donation must be held in balance, or impotence and unreality will result . . . there is an ultimate social value in the most secret responses of the soul to grace."

When we preach the gospel we preach it with our lives. We reveal our acquiescence to the claim of Jesus by what we do and what we say.

Part II of this book is a series of true stories about good people. It is offered to make the point that love in action usually takes the form of service. This is not to suggest that Christian life must always be action-oriented. But it is a fact that we teach others by our example, by our courage, our patience, our willingness to serve.

In the same way we in turn are inspired by the good example of others. Jesus went about doing good. The Christian seeks ways of imitating Him. St. Paul summed it up:

Help carry one another's burdens. In this way you will fulfill the law of Jesus Christ.   (Gal. 6:2)

* * *

I am only one
   But still I am one.
I cannot do everything
   But still I can do something.
I will not refuse to do the something
   that I can do.

                              Edward Everett Hall

The Shepherd's Masterpiece

In the late 1930s, a young traveler came upon a desolate upland region in the French Alps where nothing grew but wild lavender. There were no trees, water was scarce, villages were long deserted and the few inhabitants were primitive and hostile.

Yet the traveler met a shepherd who invited him to stay the night in a sturdy house that had been rebuilt from a ruin. The shepherd, who lived alone, puzzled his guest by taking out a sack of acorns that evening, selecting good ones in groups of 10 and discarding those which were cracked or too small. He counted 100, then went to bed.

Next day, the traveler accompanied his host on a strange journey. The shepherd, with his sack of acorns and an inch-thick iron rod about 18 inches long, climbed up to a wind-swept ridge. Again and again he plunged his rod into the desolate earth and planted an acorn in each hole. He was planting oak trees, and had been doing so for three years. He had planted about 100,000 in all, of which he expected one-tenth to survive.

The shepherd, whose name was Elzeard Bouffier, related that he had once owned a farm in the lowlands, and had retired here at the age of 50 after the death of his wife and son. He was convinced this land was dying for want of trees, and he vowed, if God gave him life, he would do something about it. And so for his remaining years, he planted trees.

Twenty-five years later, the same traveler returned to the region. It had blossomed to life. A forest, now five miles long and nearly two wide, had replaced the desolate terrain. The once dry streams were flowing again, fed by the rain and snow the forest conserves. The waters served all forms of life. Willows had reappeared; there were rushes, meadows, gardens and flowers. As streams began to flow again, young farming couples came to settle in the area. Little by little a small village developed.

Elzeard Bouffier lived to see most of it. He died in 1947 a happy man. To the world he probably seemed eccentric, but he knew he was following his own unique calling. He was true to himself; his story is a testimony to the uniqueness of every individual person.

Making a Hobby Out of Christmas

When neighbors found the body of Tony Gruttadauria in his modest apartment they were amazed to see thousands of brightly wrapped Christmas presents stacked to the ceiling all around him. The 64-year-old salesman, it was subsequently learned, spent all his savings collecting and wrapping gifts in anticipation of the Christmas celebration, when he dressed in a Santa Claus outfit and distributed gifts to needy children throughout central Florida.

Don Rothy, a friend, said, "He was always broke because he was always spending his money on toys.

"What he would do is go around to these flea markets and garage sales all year long and he'd buy up toys and anything else that had to do with Christmas...

"He didn't have much furniture—a bed, a television that didn't work properly, a radio and a few other things, and then the rest of the apartment was packed full of Christmas things, I mean to the ceiling, thousands."

"He just loved kids. He was a kid himself. He wasn't off his rocker. He just enjoyed making kids happy. This became his hobby 365 days a year."

There is something poetic about a grown man living out his last years to make children a little happier. Tony Gruttadauria's life is a modern Santa Claus parable. That same spirit which filled him with generous love touches most of us around Christmas. Wouldn't it be wonderful if we had it all year round the way Tony Gruttadauria did?

The Miracle of the Flowers

Sometimes a simple idea can turn a life around. Father James Harvey, a prison chaplain from Brooklyn, is changing many lives and he's doing it with flowers.

He saw the need for some creative intervention in the lives of neglected and rejected youngsters—those who were getting in trouble and coming before the courts as first offenders. He knew what the future would hold for them if something wasn't done to help. So he conceived an ingenious plan, an exciting non-profit program called "Flowers With Care."

He enlisted the help of a group of florists. Now, with their support and the support of skilled counsellors, the program helps these young people to learn the rudiments of business and the art of floral design.

More than 90 percent of those who have entered the program since its creation in 1974 have made good professionally, becoming florists, nursery men and women and flower shop managers. Only one of the program's graduates has gotten into further trouble.

The training program is nine months long, and it involves on-the-job guidance with experienced florists. Participants learn everything from basic botany to marketing, design, pricing and bookkeeping. The trainees range in age from 16 to 24. They receive the minimum wage at the start of the program with raises in the third and eighth month. At the end of the course, "Flowers With Care" provides for placement, giving the young people a job with a future.

The program even provides a place to live, warm clothing and medical care for those who need it. In return, there are high standards to be met.

Trainees must be drug and alcohol free and remain so. They must develop good work habits, punctuality, cooperation with fellow employees, and a readiness to follow orders. The whole thing is working so well that the courts and the school authorities now refer youngsters to Father Harvey.

How do you turn a life around? How do you give a person pride, responsibility, hope and the opportunity for economic security? Ask Father James Harvey, he's doing it. I call it the miracle of the flowers.

For Crippled Children, an Advocate

"It's a great feeling to see a child running down a corridor, after doctors have said she'd die in the first two years of her life," says Bill Ball. "She's eight now and although she can't talk, she's alive and full of vigor. The sight of a child like that makes you want to work a little harder for something you believe in and help someone other than yourself."

Five days a week Bill Ball is a transportation stock and tool attendant whose job helps maintain the light and power supplies of Syracuse, New York. But Bill's efforts after working hours have brought light into the lives of hundreds of disabled youngsters.

Several years ago he became interested in fighting the effects of cerebral palsy in children born with that crippling birth defect. Assuming the job of program chairman of his local Elks lodge, he built its fundraising campaigns around pancake breakfasts, bowl-a-thons, walk-a-thons, raffles and circuses. The lodge's fundraising climbed steadily until it led the state's 143 Elks clubs with $12,000 in one year.

"I told my wife Shirley when I first joined the lodge," Bill said, "if I couldn't make a contribution or help someone less fortunate than myself, I'd resign."

Anyone who truly loves God and neighbor will find ways to express that love, both during and after working hours. Everyone has a different gift. Bill Ball was good at raising money. What are you good at? Wherever you are, there is someone who needs what you alone can give.

'Mum Shirl' Champions Aborigines

When Mother Teresa, who ministers to the dying of Calcutta, visited Australia, it was Shirley Smith whom she wanted to meet. Known as the "black saint," Mrs. Smith is an aborigine who neither reads nor writes.

She is known as "Mum Shirl" by the 20,000 to 30,000 aborigines of Sydney. "Mum Shirl" is angry about the miserable lot of her people. She has channeled that anger into a lifetime of work on their behalf at St. Vincent's Church, working seven days a week with people beset with poor health and alcoholism. She has appeared in court on behalf of nearly 5,000 juvenile offenders, victims of broken homes.

Shirley Smith has 13 children, 41 grandchildren and two great grandchildren; but, says Father Edward Kennedy of St. Vincent's, "at least 300 children have at some step called her 'Mummy'."

"She starts things," says Father Kennedy, "and gives them a focus. She stands by the weak."

The church has been turned into a crowded community center where down-and-out alcoholics come and where people wait to die. Shirley Smith is the moving force behind the ministry of a priest, a monk and six nuns who work with these people. It was here that Mother Teresa came to admire her work.

"We are learning from Shirley," says Father Kennedy, "to know the poor and to love the poor."

A Fighter for Justice

Josie Lujan, a kindly grandmother from Monte Vista, Colorado, went back to school when her husband, a disabled veteran, could no longer work. All she wanted to be was a wife and mother but they had nine children and she had to become the breadwinner.

One of the girls was mentally handicapped. Josie called her "our exceptional child." So it was natural that in returning to school she did so with the intent of helping handicapped children. Her family gave her full support and although studying wasn't easy, she persevered. Five days after graduating from college she signed her first teaching contract.

It wasn't long before this Hispanic woman discovered that affluent suburban schools had much better books and programs than she had seen in rural schools. One day, her grandson visited her and said, "Grandma, you've got more books at home than our whole school library."

"At that moment," Josie recalls, "I knew I would have to do something." And she did.

With the help of the Chicano Education Project in Denver, she interested other parents. There were months of frustration and threatening phone calls and letters. She was accused of trying to ruin the school system. But Josie was a fighter and eventually she became the principal plaintiff in a law suit which succeeded in overturning Colorado's method of financing school districts.

State Legislator Federico Pena said, "The day Josie Lujan won her suit you would have thought the golden dome of the Capital had fallen on the Colorado Legislature... They were mad."

Josie became a member of the school board and something of a symbol of bravery for her Hispanic brothers and sisters. "We have to keep working," she said, "there's a long way to go."

Women like Josie Lujan are the life-blood of this nation. Our country was established on the principle of the equality of all persons under God. It takes vigilance and courage to make our ideals work. The Christophers believe that every individual is important and that one person can make a difference. Josie Lujan proved it.

He Became 'Grandpa' to a Whole Class

At the age of 82, Fred Brandner, a retired mathematics professor of Ames, Iowa, became a kindergarten volunteer and he loved it. Whenever he entered the classroom, the youngsters cheered and rushed for his hugs. Surrounded by the beaming children, "Grandpa Fred"—that's what the children called him—said, "This sure beats sitting around being bored."

Modern science has enabled more and more people to live to an old age. But often what should be a time of happy relaxation is marred by loneliness. But loneliness doesn't have to be part of old age. There are many alternatives to the rocking chair.

Fred Brandner picked a good one. Like so many other talented people, he went through an uncomfortable period of adjustment after his retirement. No one finds it easy to change their life pattern, but he was fortunate enough to have a Retired Senior Volunteer Program (RSVP) near his home. The local Community Preschool Center needed some volunteer help and RSVP placed him in the job.

Getting the elderly to work with youngsters is one of the best ways of helping both the young and the old. "It adds new meaning to our older citizens' lives," says David McNamara, the Ames RSVP director. "More important, it gets them back into the community and helps them feel useful again; and it helps the youngsters too. We see a lot of love and dedication in this program."

Sometimes the spiritual training of a lifetime remains

hidden like the proverbial light under a bushel basket. People have the desire and the ability but they're afraid to push themselves into the unknown. It sometimes takes a third party to show the way. That's why something like RSVP is so valuable. If you do not have such a program in your area and you think it would be useful, talk to others about it. Reading stories, helping the children in their study periods, supervising their play during recreation—these are some of the many ways senior citizens can help. They just need a little incentive, a place to serve and some creative planning.

"I'm over 80 and that doesn't seem very old to me," said Grandpa Brandner, "right now it does me a world of good to love—and be loved—by these little ones." Joy follows love.

A Special Adoption

In September of 1978, Terry Snyder adopted a nine-year-old Korean girl named Johanne Susan. Both Miss Snyder and Johanne are blind.

After months of preparation, the little girl arrived at the Philadelphia International Airport where Terry Snyder was waiting with a Korean priest, Father Thaddeus Park. Dressed in white and carrying a little doll, Johanne was led through the crowd to Miss Snyder. They embraced.

"Welcome, I love you," Miss Snyder said in Korean. She had rehearsed the words many times. "I think she's a little frightened; does she understand that I can't see either?" she asked. Father Park assured her that Johanne knew. The two remained locked in one another's arms. Terry Snyder, the director of the Catholic Guild for the Blind in New York City, was filled with happiness.

The months of paper work leading up to the adoption were all worthwhile, Miss Snyder thought. Her mind raced ahead to new challenges. "We have to teach her English before we can teach her anything else." She was asked how she planned to do it. "I'll take her from room to room and give her the English word for each object she touches in the house," she said.

As the two prepared to leave the airport, Miss Snyder again turned to Father Park and said, "Oh, Father, tell her I love her and I want her to be happy!"

It was six months after Johanne's arrival when I called Terry Snyder at her office in New York and I was pleased to learn that Johanne was already speaking English and making friends with the neighborhood children in the New Jersey suburb where she and her new mother live. I asked Terry Snyder if the responsibility had been more than she bargained for; she answered without hesitation, "Father, I think it's the best thing I've ever done. I'm so happy."

I was happy too for Terry and Johanne. The greatest treasure on earth is love; to gain love we must first give it away.

Man With a Million Friends

Twenty-five years on the same street corner was a pleasant experience for one Chicago policeman. Rarely is a policeman so long at one location. Officer James Lettner used the time to build a circle of friends with his cheerfulness while performing his duties.

"It's been a good life," he said upon retiring after directing traffic on the corner of State Street and Adams in the city's Loop for over a quarter of a century. "My wife and I put two daughters and a son through college on a cop's pay. We can't complain."

A 65-year-old newsdealer who had shared the same corner commented, "Jimmy Lettner is the greatest guy who ever lived. He must have a million friends. He's always helping mothers with babies or small children, older people and handicapped people across the street. He takes care not to embarrass them—he just walks alongside them mostly."

Love and good cheer go together. More than a century ago, Thomas Carlyle, the English historian, said: "Wondrous is the strength of cheerfulness and its power of endurance. The cheerful man will do more in the same time, will do it better, will persevere in it longer, than the sad or sullen."

Good cheer is universally praised:

■ "A cheerful heart has a continual feast." (Prov. 15:15)

■ "The plainest sign of wisdom is a continual cheerfulness." (Michel de Montaigne, 1580)

■ "A light heart lives long." (Shakespeare, 1595)

■ "Cheerfulness keeps up a kind of daylight in the mind." (Joseph Addison, 1712)

■ "We ought to be as cheerful as we can, if only because to be happy ourselves is a most effectual contribution to the happiness of others." (John Lubbock, 1890)

Love and joy and cheer are inseparable companions.

Community Journalism at Its Best

It was the summer of 1979 when a significantly high number of cases of intestinal flu were treated in Bradford, Pennsylvania. City manager Pat Nuzzo couldn't offer any explanations. That wasn't good enough for reporter Katherine Nichols of the Bradford Journal, a weekly newspaper.

She dug into the story and discovered that the local

pharmacies had dispensed 1,050 prescriptions for drugs to treat giardia, an intestinal disorder. Her story led to public demands for an explanation. It was learned that several doctors at the Bradford hospital had met earlier but decided not to inform the public so as to avoid panic.

It was not until late September that legal notice was given that coliform was found in the water; coliform is a sign of contamination.

The Bradford Journal informed the people of the danger to health, and urged them to boil the water. City officials minimized the problem and attacked the Journal. The paper reported that cases of giardiosis were diagnosed as early as July but were not reported. In October the Journal brought the issue to a head with a special edition. Its warnings probably saved hundreds of residents from infection. However, subsequent tests conducted by federal and state laboratories seemed to disprove the contamination theory and many people, thinking that the water was pure again, stopped boiling it.

Katherine Nichols and the Journal stepped in again. They interviewed an official of the Disease Control Center in Atlanta, who advised continued caution because in his judgment the negative test results were not conclusive. Finally a health emergency was declared, and steps were taken to clear up the problem. A possible public health disaster was prevented.

What can one person do? One person with courage and determination can stop an epidemic.

One Man's Courage United a Country

Canada's new national hero is Terry Fox, who died of cancer after showing the world a rare kind of courage. He captured the imagination of millions of his countrymen with a self-styled Marathon of Hope. Terry, who nearly four years before his death lost a leg to bone cancer, pledged that he would run across Canada to raise funds for cancer research.

Little attention was paid to him at first. He began on April 12, 1980, at St. John's, Newfoundland, intending to run 5,170 miles to Vancouver, British Columbia. By the time a month had passed, it became clear that the young dreamer on a wooden leg was actually doing what he said he would.

I was caught up in the excitement surrounding his run when I vacationed in Ontario that summer. The media began following his every move and his countrymen rallied to the cause, contributing millions of dollars to cancer research.

Terry ran an average of 24 miles a day for 142 consecutive days, but he collapsed on Sept. 1 at Thunder Bay, Ontario, 3,339 miles from the start. His chest was aching, his breathing labored; the doctors found that his cancer had spread to his lungs. They rushed him to his home town of Port Coquitlam, British Columbia, for chemotherapy.

What followed was an unbelievable outpouring of emotions and charitable contributions; nearly $20 million from all over Canada. Every province was involved and traditional divisions dissolved. One telethon was put together in 48 hours and more than $10 million was raised on that show alone.

Terry Fox created a spirit of national unity unparalleled in Canadian history. In a bi-lingual, fractious nation of 23.7 million people, this unknown dreamer inspired a new national pride.

The Christophers stress the importance of one person over and again. Terry is a marvelous example of what one person can do. He began alone, trying to raise money for cancer research; today he is remembered as a national symbol of courage and determination.

Making the Punishment Fit the Crime

On a recent Christopher Closeup TV program, we interviewed Judge Dennis Challeen of Winona, Minnesota, on the topic of "positive sentencing." In his court, Judge Challeen requires the criminal to pay back what he has taken or destroyed. This is an attempt not only to make restitution but to make the criminal feel like a worthwhile human being, who isn't hated, but who is part of the community and accountable to the community for his actions.

Statistics indicate that more than half of the 200,000 men and women behind bars at this moment will return to prison sometime after their release, usually for more serious crimes. It costs taxpayers approximately $27,000 per year for each criminal behind bars.

Judge Challeen admits that some people have to be imprisoned. But he questions the wisdom of a system which isn't really rehabilitating criminals. Not only that, it isn't really protecting citizens because criminals come out of jail angrier and more dangerous than ever. Worst of all the present system does nothing to compensate the victim of the crime.

I asked Judge Challeen how he would handle a man who went on a drunken spree and crashed his car into someone's front porch. The judge replied:

"We have a victim, don't we? He owes the owner of the house something. He caused the police to come into play, the courts, the probation officers. He owes society something for that.

"But worst of all is the fact that he probably has a serious drinking problem. We want to work on all three aspects.

"I would probably lock him up for a short spell. He would pay a fine. Then I would release him to work and turn over part of his paycheck to the owner of the damaged house. I might also require some kind of treatment if he is an alcoholic."

Judge Challeen is doing something different with our criminal justice system, and people are beginning to listen to him. It proves again that one person can make a difference.

A Lesson in Loving

One person can make a significant difference in the lives of others, even if that person is severely handicapped. Let me tell you about Oliver. He was the second of six children born to my friends, Catherine and Jose de Vinck. Oliver was brain-damaged and multi-handicapped from birth: blind, mute and paralyzed.

Two doctors said he would not live beyond his fifth birthday, but they didn't count on the extent of his family's love and devotion. He lived until March 12, 1980, a month before his 33rd birthday. I had the honor of preaching at his funeral and I remember the feelings that I tried to put into words:

"There is much that I've learned from Oliver's meekness and poverty," I said. "Other than his bed and his box of diapers, he never owned anything. His life reminded me of the Tolstoy short story, *What Men Live By*. In a world where money and possessions are regarded as the only real security, Oliver's life gave testimony to the truth that we really live by love. In this Oliver was rich. He was hand-fed every spoonful of food he ever ate.

"His body was unblemished. Since his back never left the sheets beneath him (he was rigid and could not be turned on his side) it took constant care to protect him from the bed sores that plague bed-ridden patients.

"Life is not always thought of as sacred (there are

about 40 to 50 million abortions performed in the world each year) but Oliver's family regarded his life as a priceless gift. So just by his silent presence Oliver taught me about the sacredness of life.

"Oliver also taught me about service, the deeper meaning of it. Yet he never really did anything for anyone. He was not a doer in the ordinary sense of the word, but he served those around him by helping them grow in love, wisdom, perseverance, kindness, patience and fidelity. For those who served him, Oliver's life gave special meaning to the words of Jesus: 'What you did for the least of My brethren, you did for Me.'

"I learned from Oliver that the meek and humble do us a great service by evoking from us our best love. Oliver made his brothers and sisters strong and generous human beings.

"Oliver showed me the beauty of innocence. He was never jealous, resentful, deceitful; he never hurt anyone. He kept all the commandments, and excelled in the fourth commandment. He honored his mother and father. We usually think people honor their parents by their accomplishments. Parents take pride in the successes of their children, graduation, worldly honors, financial success. But Oliver honored his parents in a different way by revealing them to us. He showed us the kind of people they are, and we honor them on this day of Oliver's funeral.

"And now it is over. A love story, 33 years in the making. Now the de Vincks have one of their own, a saint in heaven. Oliver is free at last, free from the confinement of his own body. He now has all eternity to laugh and dance in the fullness of life."

Can a broken life such as Oliver's be the source of great joy in a family? Ask the de Vincks and the millions of others who have said "yes" to God in similar cases. Joy does prevail over sorrow.

Bit by Bit, a Better World

"I can't change the whole world, but I can try to change a small part of it," said Mrs. Kay Fiorentino of San Pedro, California. That's a Christopher statement if I ever heard one, so I'm going to tell you a little about her.

She is an extraordinary woman who started a crusade against pornography in San Pedro a few years ago. She closed down an X-rated movie house, an "adult" bookstore dealing in sex-explicit materials, and a house of prostitution.

"It wasn't easy," she says. "It took 69 days of continuous picketing day and night in the latter part of 1975 to close down the Mermaid Theater."

It was during the picketing that the owner of an X-rated bookstore across the street put up a sign defying the picketers: "Ninth Anniversary! Thank you, San Pedro." It was like waving a red flag, so Mrs. Fiorentino's Citizens Opposed to Pornography (COP) chose the bookstore as its second target. Again it took more than two months of daily picketing but the owner finally closed that store and two others nearby.

It all began when a priest at St. Peter's Catholic Church, aware of her organizational abilities, appealed to her to help him do something about the porno theater in town.

"What's a 'porno' theater?" she asked.

"When I found out, that's when I started to do something about it," she said later.

She had to retire from Lockheed in Burbank at the age of 39 because of rheumatoid arthritis. Left to her pain and idleness, she got worse. Her world ended.

"For five years I just existed. Life had no meaning for me." But once she became involved in the community, she recalls now, "life began to take on new meaning. I became physically active and that was good for me."

Her husband Gerrard, who operates a commercial fishing boat supply store, gave his wife of 21 years his full support. He believes it was all in God's plan and so does she.

Kay Fiorentino minimizes her own strength and tenacity. She gives the 150 members of COP, two Catholic parishes and members of the local Mormon Church a large part of the credit for the victorious struggle.

"Looking back I cannot help but believe it was God's will that I do it and I'm happy I could," she says.

Kay Fiorentino and her husband endured harassment, ridicule and scorn for their efforts. They think it was worth it.

CHAPTER NINE

Heroes of Yesterday

In the next few pages I'm going to take you back in time to consider some outstanding people of yesterday — people who also have made a difference.

Our first story takes place just after World War II. In September, 1944, Group Captain Leonard Cheshire received England's Victoria Cross for heroism, becoming the most decorated man in the Royal Air Force. After the war, a friend named Arthur Dykes came to him in need. Dykes was dying of cancer; he had no place to go, and no way to support himself.

The retired group captain owned a run-down country home, so he decided to take Dykes in and care for him there. It was a long ordeal but before Dykes died, he expressed a thought which lingered in Cheshire's mind. He said that he had the feeling he had been sent there for a purpose and not merely to be cared for. Those words from a dying man proved to be prophetic.

Why not dedicate myself to this work, Cheshire

thought? Why not take in others as helpless as Arthur? Why should their days end in cold and lonely hospital wards?

But where would the money come from? Cheshire rose to the challenge. His Christian faith gave him the courage to make a decision he never regretted. "If patients turn up, we'll take them. We won't worry about money—we'll leave everything to God's Providence."

Surprising things seem to happen to human beings who have the faith to trust God's Providence, as the RAF hero soon learned.

One after another they began to arrive: the dying, the severely disabled, the poor. Almost overnight the old house was filled to overflowing. When there was no more money to carry on, gifts seemed to appear just when needed.

The multiplication of the loaves was a stunning miracle, and Cheshire was chosen for another spectacular miracle —the multiplication of the homes.

Cheshire Home No. 2 was started in Cornwall. By 1955, Cheshire Homes were in India, Malaya, Nigeria, Jordan, Hong Kong, Ethiopia and Portugal. Today, the Cheshire Foundation is truly international with about 170 homes in 32 countries. There are four in the U.S. Patients in these homes pay what they can afford but inability to pay does not bar them.

In an age when more and more consideration is being given to the problems of the sick and elderly, Leonard Cheshire showed the way. He proved once again that one person, with faith in God's Holy Providence, can perform wonders. But in every instance it takes the leap of faith which overcomes all fear.

A Man Who Persevered

I always liked the story of Thomas Edison's persevering nature. Once he was working with an assistant who, in a fit of frustration, exclaimed, "We should give up. We've gone through thousands of experiments and they've all failed." Edison turned to him and said, "Failed no, we've learned several thousand things that don't work . . . we're getting closer."

On Oct. 19, 1879, Edison lit a light bulb that burned for 40 hours: Later he developed one that lasted 102 hours. For him, "perseverance" was the only way to guarantee success. For his assistant, "perseverance" was just so much wasted energy. The way you look at something can make all the difference. Vince Lombardi, the great football coach of the Green Bay Packers, once said, "A winner never quits, and a quitter never wins." Edison wasn't a quitter.

Human judgment is so often clouded by feelings. We judge events, other people and even ourselves not so much on the objective facts but on the basis of our private feelings. Edison's assistant didn't want to fail. He was just tired. He wanted to rest. He wanted to call it quits.

Lots of people get tired. They get tired of their marriage, of their profession, of their religion. They get tired of being good, tired of striving, tired of giving, tired of praying.

The real danger is not in getting tired, the real danger is in the temptation to quit. Such desires are born of pessimism and cynicism. Tiredness can add to the burden, but it doesn't defeat us. Cynicism is the enemy. Cynicism is from the dark side of the human spirit. Perseverance is born of hope.

The man who lit the first light bulb persevered. He lit more than one little bulb—he lit up the whole world. And even more than that he taught us a lesson in courage. I'm inclined to believe that the lesson was at least as important a contribution as the light bulb.

The General Was a Gentleman

Speaking well of those who disliked him was one of Gen. Robert E. Lee's outstanding qualities. When he paid generous tribute to the ability of a certain colleague, a fellow officer remarked: "General, how can you speak so highly of one of your bitterest enemies, a man who never misses an opportunity to malign you?"

"My friend," Lee replied, "the President asked my opinion of him, not his opinion of me."

Robert E. Lee was a man of dignity. His self-discipline in speech is worthy of emulation. Speaking well of others in all circumstances was a practice he began early in life. Only after years of practice does such a state of mind become habitual. It takes determination to develop nobility of character.

By cultivating the habit of thinking and speaking well of others, regardless of their attitude towards you, you make an investment that will one day bear rich dividends, not only here, but hereafter.

It is a sign of strength rather than weakness to follow Christ's teaching: "Love your enemies, do good to those that hate you and pray for those who persecute and calumniate you." (Mt. 5:44)

General Lee was not on the winning side of the American Civil War but he is remembered with love and respect for his extraordinary character.

Maria Montessori: Innovator

Have you ever gotten one of your best ideas, a real breakthrough in your thinking, when you felt you were at your lowest point? Well it happened to Maria Montessori in 1894.

Born in Italy in 1870, Maria was the first woman in

Italian history admitted to medical school. Her fellow students were hostile. She often had to work late and alone, in buildings that were cold and badly lit.

As the pressure mounted she became so depressed that one night she decided to abandon her career; medicine, she thought, was no place for a woman. That night she walked dejectedly through a local park only to be distracted by the pathetic sight of a beggar woman sleeping on a bench. Next to the woman on the cold ground was a child playing peacefully with a long, red ribbon.

How could it be, Maria wondered, that a piece of ribbon could keep a poor, neglected child occupied and happy? Maria was moved deeply. Suddenly a vision came to her, she knew she had to finish her medical studies in order to help deprived children.

In 1896 she graduated, and soon developed a technique to teach retarded children. It was so successful that in 1899 Dr. Montessori was invited to speak at a teachers' congress in Turin. She electrified her audience with the claim that retarded children could be trained and should be given a chance at education.

Maria Montessori hated to see pupils in class "sitting like rows of butterflies transfixed with a pin." Her system is based on the premise that children want to learn. In the Montessori method the teacher supervises from a distance, giving help only when it's asked for or needed. Children are allowed to move around freely and choose what they want to do, providing they preserve good manners and refrain from disturbing the classroom harmony.

Her idea worked so well with exceptional children that she began to develop it for universal application. "Little by little," Dr. Montessori said, "I became convinced that similar methods applied to normal children would develop and set free their personalities in a marvelous and surprising way."

Maria Montessori lived to be 82. Long before her death in 1952 she had the joy and satisfaction of seeing her educational theories and techniques vindicated. Her method has helped millions of people. One educator changed their world.

The First Woman of Letters

This story is about Elena Cornaro, who in 1678 became the first woman ever to earn a doctoral degree.

Prelates and scholars traveled great distances to be at Padua University, Italy, for the graduation of the 32-year-old Venetian woman. "She was as beautiful as an angel," Professor Carlo Rinaldini wrote in his diary, "and she spoke Greek, Latin, French and Spanish with perfect ease." He had the honor of placing the laurel crown on her head, the doctor's ring on her finger and the teacher's ermine cape on her shoulders. Elena was a trail blazer.

Elena's father was both wealthy and influential. When he first asked Cardinal Gregorio Barbarigo, bishop of Padua and chancellor of the university, to enroll his daughter in the doctoral program, the churchman laughed, saying, "We would be held up to the mockery of the world."

Eventually, however, the cardinal recognized her special talents and enrolled her to study for a degree in philosophy. In spite of all the prejudices of her male classmates, Elena persevered and excelled in her studies. She mastered philosophy, theology, mathematics and astronomy.

Unfortunately, after her graduation she contracted tuberculosis and had to leave the damp climate of Venice and return to Padua where she spent her time caring for the needy as a Benedictine Oblate lay parish worker. Her death came at an early age of 38.

What I find so moving in Elena's story is that the first woman to achieve academic equality with men on her own merits was holy. She involved herself with those who needed her help, the poor people in her home town. Elena Cornaro used the talents God gave her not merely to gain honors for herself but more importantly to care for others.

A Contemporary Saint

Dorothy Day was another holy woman. She worked out her holiness on the streets of New York City and died there just before Christmas, 1980. She practiced voluntary poverty and was a writer, a fighter for justice, a pacifist, a mother, and above all a woman of prayer.

At her wake, hundreds of people gathered to pay their respects. As she lay there in an open pine box, as poor in death as she was in life, I stood nearby filled with awe at the sight of her. There was no attempt to disguise the reality of death. No make-up, no fancy fabric. In spite of her discolored skin, her face had a stark and luminous beauty about it. The remains of Dorothy Day were in that room, but Dorothy was with God.

Years before, as a college student at Fordham University, I had discovered *The Catholic Worker*, the monthly paper she published. Her ideas hit me like an electric shock. I thought I knew what Christianity was all about until I was confronted with her concept of voluntary poverty. She had renounced all her possessions to live among the poor, feeding them and clothing them. She lived the Sermon on the Mount so radically that it made thousands of readers re-examine their entire value system.

Catherine de Hueck Doherty, the foundress of Madonna House in Ontario, Canada, another great woman in her own right, tells a story about the time she and Dorothy Day were working among the poorest of the poor in New York City many years ago. One night the women's dorm was so crowded there wasn't even space on the floor.

When the last stranger came in looking for warmth and a place to sleep, Dorothy said, "It's all right, let her in, she can sleep with me."

With that Catherine called Dorothy aside and said, "Can't you see that woman is in the last stages of syphilis?" Without hesitation, Dorothy replied, "That is not a woman with syphilis, for me she is Jesus Christ."

For Dorothy Day, religion was not a system of cultural beliefs inherited from one's parents. It was a commitment to Jesus and His teachings. She lived her ideals, but she never did it with an air of superiority. Practicing the works of mercy, opposing war, running a soup kitchen in New York's Bowery, witnessing to the love of Jesus. That was her life. For her it was as natural as breathing.

Once a TV interviewer asked her what words she would like on her tombstone. She answered without hesitation: "Deo Gratias."

Christians believe that holiness is possible. Dorothy has proven it. Her fidelity to God's grace, combined with her extraordinary calling, produced a life of legendary holiness. Her "Deo Gratias" testifies to the joy that was in her heart. Such joy does not come without some sacrifice.

In Chinatown, a Jewish Angel

Like Dorothy Day, Rose Livingston lived an extraordinary vocation among the victims of life in New York City, barging into the city's dives and speakeasies in the 20s and 30s to rescue young girls from white slavers and pimps. Sleeping days and working nights, she was called "The Angel of Chinatown," although she was also a familiar figure around Greenwich Village, the Brooklyn Navy Yard and other areas of the city.

The youngsters she pulled from the bars and the taverns she took into her home instead of turning them over to the children's society or the police. She worked to rehabilitate them and contacted their parents if possible.

Convicted white slavers attacked her repeatedly. She was beaten more than 20 times. She was stabbed and shot at, and once a gang threw her down the stairs, breaking both her legs. Another time, attackers fractured her jaw.

"But she always bounced back," remembers an admiring settlement house worker. "They say she rescued over 800 girls in the 30 years she was at it. She took her life in her hands every time she went into one of those joints."

Rose Livingston lived to be 99 years old, staying always in the same tiny apartment near New York's East River. When she died in 1976, friends had both the traditional Jewish service and a Catholic Mass for her, explaining that "Rose would understand that."

Fighting against social evils has never been safe or easy. Real accomplishment often means sacrifice of personal safety. It can even mean the loss of life. But people like Rose Livingston, who saved 800 teenage girls, would say it's worth it.

CHAPTER TEN

Overcoming Fear

Rejoice in the Lord always, again I say rejoice... The Lord is at hand. Have no anxiety about anything.

(Phil. 4:4)

The challenge of Paul has always intrigued me. Not only does he tell us not to worry about anything, he tells us to rejoice—always. It seems a bit farfetched when you consider the problems he was enduring himself. Here was a man facing trial and the danger of bodily punishment. He had been flogged and beaten before, and he had seen cruel executions. Yet Paul, like so many in the stories you've just read, seems to have managed to put aside natural fears.

What I find particularly interesting is that he makes a definite connection between the dismissal of anxiety and the presence of joy. He is not telling us to banish fear and then rejoice. Banishing fear isn't that simple anyway. But he is saying, "Rejoice in the Lord... have no anxiety about anything."

He puts the decision to rejoice first. Do you know why? Because the spirit of joy tempers our fears. We may not be able to eliminate all feelings of fear by a simple act of the will, but by controlling our thoughts we can deal with them constructively.

Concentrating on God's love and protection can help prevent undue psychological anxiety.

Rejoicing because of the knowledge of God's love is in itself a kind of exorcism. St. Paul knew that anxiety does not flourish in the atmosphere of joy. He prescribes joy as a means of banishing anxiety. Our faith in the reality of God's love is of great benefit in healing and liberating the fearful spirit.

Rejoicing in the Lord is the work of the Holy Spirit. When Jesus says, "Be not afraid," He is asking us to trust Him.

What is fear?

Fear is an inner disturbance caused by some anticipated danger, real or imagined. We react from danger defensively in anger, resentment, hatred; sometimes with violence. Because of this, fear is an enemy of love and the antithesis of joy. Joy is driven out by fear.

But let's distinguish between real fear and worry. Worry is a mild form of fear. We all know that a responsible person has some legitimate worry. All normal people worry about their responsibilities, the things they have to do to make life more meaningful for themselves and others. Worry is part of the human condition. Whenever we engage in some form of planning for a future event, whether it's a vacation, a wedding, a new job or a trip to the dentist, we worry. Worry is normal and necessary to healthy living.

But real fear is more than worry; fear immobilizes. It is the dreaded enemy of the soul.

I once spoke to Dorothy Day about fear. "Fear is one

of the most dangerous things. To get over fears and teach your children to get over fears is very hard," she said. "Fear causes you to criticize a lot, you end up with a chip on your shoulder. You start something in retaliation and you end up getting hurt, and partly it's your own fault."

She continued, "Fear ruins your perspective; fear is what makes the police trigger-happy. There's a terrible fear of the whites for the blacks and the blacks for the whites, and there shouldn't be. All people everywhere are really only demanding that they be treated like human beings."

In the spirit of Jesus who said, "Learn of Me for I am meek and gentle of heart," Dorothy Day learned to love the poor and the downtrodden. She was never fearful in their presence.

Most people cannot reach out to the poor because they are afraid of them; afraid of their neighborhoods, even afraid of their children. When fear begins to breed division, it becomes a spiritual problem. We are victims of our own fears when we allow them to shape our decisions and our personality.

The Lord calls us to forgiveness, peace, and humility, but our fears lead us to hatred, vindictiveness, arrogance, and confrontation. Jean Vanier once said, "We are afraid of the person in misery because he constitutes a danger to us. His poverty and his needs challenge our riches. So we raise the barriers to keep him from our sight."

As the son of a former Canadian Governor General, Vanier might have had a brilliant career in government, but instead he devoted himself to helping the mentally handicapped by living among them in a small house in France and serving them on a daily basis. With a small staff he has made a home for a dozen or so retarded and handicapped young adults. It is not an institution but a home, a family of loved ones, where one and all share their meals and dreams.

In his book, *Be Not Afraid,* published by Griffen House, Toronto, 1975, he said, "I have learned more about the gospels from handicapped people, those on the margins of our society, those who have been crushed and hurt, than I have from the wise and prudent. Through their own acceptance and surrender, wounded people have taught me that I must learn to accept my weakness and not pretend to be strong and capable. Handicapped people have shown me how handicapped I am, how handicapped we all are."

Jean Vanier reminds us all how much we need to learn from the meek and the humble of this world. It is only when we accept our own littleness that we can learn to open ourselves to the Spirit of Love which Jesus promised.

I value human beings like Jean Vanier who show us the way of love. We are so afraid to take on the burdens of love, even though we know love purifies us and makes us whole. Love is the highest challenge of life. It is the ticket to heaven; the secret of a joyful life.

St. John of the Cross once said, "When the evening of this life comes we will be judged on love."

Centuries later, another great teacher repeated this theme: "Each one has a mission to fulfill, a mission of love. At the hour of death when we come face to face with God, we are going to be judged on love; not how much we have done, but how much love we have put into the doing." The words are those of Mother Teresa of Calcutta.

How does it work in practice? Let me answer with a story.

A young pre-med student was spending some time in Latin America. Seeing a small girl cold and shivering in a thin dress, with little prospect for decent meals, he questioned God's love for His people. How could God allow it? But suddenly he realized she would feel God's love only if he himself did something to help her. He recognized the great truth: Love can only pass from person to person.

Charity is at the heart of Christian perfection, charity is human love. Love flows from person to person or it doesn't flow at all. It is not communicated by institutions or organizations but by the people who comprise them. Love can only be communicated in what we do or say or feel for another person. But too often, fear gets in the way; fear of the unknown, fear of danger, fear of loss. Fear stops us from loving. We put our own safety first and freeze up with our questions. Without love in our hearts, we fail to teach as Christ did, we fail to love as He loved.

When fear takes over, people begin to cop out: Why should I stick my neck out? What if it backfires? Who knows what could happen? Why should I get involved?

So we hold back, crippled by anxiety. The devil wins again. The Book of Proverbs says: "Better is an open rebuke than a love that remains hidden."

There are many reasons we fail to love: pride, anger, jealousy, envy, lust, sloth, gluttony. We get too wrapped up in ourselves. Fear does it to us. Every one of the vices produces a harvest of misery that can all be traced to fear in one way or another. Let's look at how fear keeps us from becoming happier persons; let's take a closer look at the vices which work against charity.

Pride is an excessive love of self which eventually leads to an abhorrence of others. Everyone else is considered beneath one's own dignity. Pride is rooted in the fear of losing one's superiority, whether it be in rank, wealth, talent, beauty or reputation. Pretending to be superior goes hand in hand with the fear of failure. When pride suppresses love, it leads to disaster. Prides goes before the fall.

Anger, whether suppressed or expressed in a rage, is the strong emotion of displeasure. It is the result of not getting what you want. Here again the fear of being deprived causes inner turmoil. The fear of being hurt in any way enflames anger.

Envy is a feeling of sadness at the good fortune of another. Here is another true enemy of happiness. It is sometimes accompanied by a degree of hatred, but it always stems from the fear of being overlooked or surpassed. Envy is a kind of habitual unhappiness. It blinds one to God's love.

Sloth is both the disinclination to action or labor, and the attachment to rest and quiet. The slothful person does not want to give up his comfort. The fear of being disturbed makes the slothful person extremely secretive and lonely. Sloth leads to selfishness. Love withers in a slothful person.

Lust is an inordinate desire for the gratification of one's sexual appetite. It is self-absorbed and crushes true love. Eventually other persons are treated like objects or worse, like slaves. In the beginning it is manifested as a fear of being alone, left without love, or intimate consolation. Later the ember bursts into flame and becomes unbridled lust, crushing all love. Consider the alternative: purity.

Purity is the virtue that is most ridiculed. It is associated with impotence, narrowness of spirit and fear of life, while in fact it is the liberating power which opens the doors of true freedom, peace and joy.

Freedom begins to vanish when self-interest becomes the consuming passion. A spirit limited to the narrow preoccupation of immediate satisfaction is ever restless, fearful of being deprived. In its most severe state, self-absorption becomes an addiction.

Purity, on the other hand, opens a person to real freedom. "Blessed are the pure in heart, for they shall see God." The really pure of heart are single-minded, they seek God above all else and they love Him not for what He can do for them but for what He is in Himself. They are capable of seeing all things as extensions of God. His beauty pervades their entire life. "In Him" they "live and breathe" and have their being. They enjoy the reflection of His beauty without feeling the need to subjugate it.

Purity opens the doors of peace because it overcomes selfish fear. A clean conscience is its own reward. Purity produces a fountain of joy; self-respect gives the soul constant delight. Those who strive for purity know that the daily struggle involves the cross. But by God's grace they also know that the cross is good. "Blessed are those who hunger and thirst for holiness, for they shall have their fill."

Jealousy is an unpleasant feeling of suspicion or resentment arising from fear or mistrust of another. Jealous people are always afraid of losing someone or something, and they become irrational, bringing misery to all concerned. Fear often seems to signal the presence of some external danger. But the real danger is from within. What is more dangerous than your own jealousy, your own anger, your lust, your greed, and all the other defects that keep you from being a loving person?

All your vices can be related to your fears; and fear is the enemy of happiness. The evil one stirs up our fears to keep us suspicious, self-centered, immobile and full of self-pity. In this way Satan tries to put us in hell day by day.

But we were made for heaven. There is always grace to help us get to the place God wants us to be. Grace is the communication of God's love, and Jesus is the mediator of divine grace.

Jesus has come to save us.
Jesus is the Lord of life and happiness.
Jesus is the Way, the Truth, and the Life.
Jesus comes to take away our fears.

* * *

As a Christian you are still human; so fears will come. But once you identify the specific brand of fear that keeps you from achieving holiness and happiness, you are in a better position to confront and conquer it, with God's help.

There are no easy answers to these complex problems, but with respect to fear here are a few ideas that may help you to cope better.

First, turn your fears over to the Lord. Study yourself and try to name the fear that most troubles you. When emotional discomfort begins, fight for self-control, calm yourself. Use the reflex principle of calling on the Lord in times of stress. The frequent repetition of a familiar prayer can be of help: "The Lord is my refuge and strength, I will not fear," (Ps. 46:1-2), or "Jesus, be my strength." Make up your own prayer to meet your specific needs.

He is the Vine, you are the branches. Simply advert to His Presence and give Him your fear. Hear His words, "Be not afraid." They are spoken to you every minute of every day. Repeated over and over again, the name of Jesus is a direct challenge to the inner disturbance of fear.

Calling upon the Lord for help has some immediate advantages. It helps you to remember that you are not alone, that you have within you God's infinite strength and love.

Next, take action; do something positive. Don't let fear immobilize you. Resist it through some loving action.

Sometimes you can take a positive action simply by not running or cowering.

I remember a woman who had that kind of courage. She was a mild-mannered 42-year-old black woman who boarded a bus in Montgomery, Alabama, on Dec. 1, 1955, and quietly sat down. In that action she set in motion a sequence of events that led to a profound change in American life.

The bus driver ordered Mrs. Rosa Parks to yield her seat to a white man and to move to the rear which was by law assigned to blacks. She didn't make a scene. She didn't threaten or exhort. She simply didn't move. She resisted her own fears and sat still. Of course, Mrs. Parks was arrested, jailed and subsequently brought to trial.

Mrs. Parks' arrest was the last straw for a 27-year-old clergyman named Martin Luther King, Jr. Dr. King organized a bus boycott which lasted 382 days. That confrontation with civil authorities culminated on Dec. 13, 1956, in a U.S. Supreme Court ruling that Alabama laws requiring segregated seating on public conveyances were unconstitutional.

Dr. King became a prophet for black people in America. The black community became aware of its strength because of his leadership, and he became aware of his mission because of Mrs. Parks, a simple seamstress from Alabama who decided not to be afraid any more. She disobeyed the "Jim Crow" laws which discriminated against her people.

"It wasn't a good feeling," she said of her arrest. "I knew anything could happen." In fact her husband, a barber, became ill from the pressure. The family ultimately moved to Detroit. Fear took its toll, but she was not overcome.

Martin Luther King once called Rosa Parks "the great fuse that led to the modern stride toward freedom."

You can decide to act against your fears too, and when you do, amazing things could begin to happen. People will notice your courage. They may even imitate you.

There will always be moments of fear for you and me. There has only been one, perfect Christian. Jesus Christ was His name, and even He experienced fear. As wounded creatures striving to be transformed in His love, we may not succeed perfectly in overcoming all our fears, but with His help we can improve mightily.

We can move beyond most fears; we can accept His amazing grace, and allow Him to transform us so as to share with us more completely His own perfect joy.

* * *

Love is a basket of bread
  from which to eat
   for years to come.
Good loaves
fragrant and warm
   miraculously multiplied;
the basket never empty
   the bread never stale.

Catherine de Vinck
A Time to Gather

CHAPTER ELEVEN

Conclusion

Rejoice with those who rejoice and be sad with those who sorrow. Treat everyone with equal kindness, never be condescending but make real friends with the poor. Do not allow yourself to become self-satisfied. Never repay evil with evil, but let everyone know you are interested in the highest ideals.

(Rom. 12:15)

The new Catholic Encyclopedia defines joy in the strict sense as "a pleasant state of quiescence in which the will rests satisfied in a good object (thing, person, action) that has been desired and is now possessed or has been accomplished."

This type of rational joy is distinguished from "delight" (delectio) which can be experienced by non-rational creatures. Humans too can delight in a good meal, or a cool breeze on a hot summer day, but "delectio" is not joy strictly speaking.

In St. Paul, joy is defined as one of the fruits of the Holy Spirit.

But the fruit of the Spirit is charity, joy, peace, patience, benignity, goodness, and perseverance.

(Gal. 5:22)

The word "fruit" is used to denote the end product of a process, the result of some prior action. Joy therefore is something that is the result of human actions performed under the influence of the Holy Spirit, causing "a certain intimate delight in the soul of the doer." Who can describe such subtle pleasures?

I won't even try, but I will draw your attention to the fact that there is a counterfeit joy or delight which can result from the attainment of an immoral goal or object. For instance, the self-satisfied feeling of a thief who uses stolen money to luxuriate at an expensive tropical hotel. But this is a flawed contentment. He is always in danger of being caught and even if he has suppressed his conscience, one day he will face some form of reckoning.

All our virtues flow from the grace of God. Our cooperation in His plan enables us to bring fulfillment to the mission He has entrusted to us. Joy flowers from this surrender to His will. We enjoy the good fruits we produce. We reap what we sow.

Each one of us grows at a different pace. God calls us and in the degree we are willing to follow Him we will bear good fruit, fruit that will last for all eternity. He has promised it. The wonderful part of all this is that it's never too late to begin, never too late to recover from a lapse. Pray for a joyful heart.

Joy has many dimensions:

■The peace of a clear conscience.

■The satisfaction of working toward the completion of one's task in life.

■The comfort of receiving human love in return for the love we have given.

■The good feeling of knowing we have helped rather than hindered our neighbor.

■The ability to celebrate life wholeheartedly in gratitude for God's many gifts.

■The security of knowing God is blessing us always and forever.

■The delight in anticipating an eternity of happiness with God.

All sacrifices and mortifications pale next to the joy God puts in the heart of those who love Him. "Rejoice in the Lord, rejoice, again I say rejoice."

Yes, the greatest honor we can give to Almighty God is to live gladly because of the knowledge of His love. Live gladly. Offer your joy along with the homage of your being to Almighty God.

As I come to the end of this book, I wish you joy. Pray for me; I will pray for you.

Never be discouraged by your faults and failings. God is good. The fact that you are reading this particular book is a sign of your special favor, a sign of His love and grace working in you, and a sign of your own good faith.

Don't be afraid if you do not yet know the taste of deep joy. Such a flower takes time to blossom. Be patient, you're not finished yet. The Lord will tend the garden of your soul, caring for you today, tomorrow and always. His love for you will never fail; He is Unchanging Love. He will give you strength to bear all your crosses, so try to put aside your worries and fears and gently learn to enjoy life as God would have you enjoy it.

Spiritual joy is not a self-conscious gift. It cannot be analyzed easily in psychological terms. One does not experience it by cultivating an optimistic outlook, or by disciplining oneself to positive thinking. Thought control doesn't produce joy. Joy is much more than a good personality or a bright disposition; more than an emotionally healthy state of mind. Anyone can experience good mental health. The gift of joy blossoms out of a compassionate heart. Joy and compassion can coexist with personal grief, suffering—one's own or that of another; it can even survive what the world calls failure. This is not to say that bad feelings are denied or suppressed; they are simply put in perspective and endured.

Compassion is not an easy virtue, but it is basic to Christian life. It produces an abundance of good fruit: joy, peace and love.

Seek first His kingdom and His righteousness, and all these things will be yours as well.

(Mt. 6:33)